# Britain's Bomb

# Britain's Bomb: What Next?

*Edited by*

## Brian Wicker
## and Hugh Beach

scm press

© Brian Wicker and contributors 2006

British Library Cataloguing in Publication data

A catalogue record for this book is available
from the British Library


0 334 04096 596 5/978 0 334 04096 5


First published in 2006 by SCM Press
9–17 St Alban's Place,
London N1 0NX

www.scm-canterburypress.co.uk

SCM Press is a division of
SCM-Canterbury Press Ltd


Printed and bound in Great Britain by
William Clowes Ltd, Beccles, Suffolk

# Contents

# Contributors

**Sir Hugh Beach** joined the Royal Engineers in August 1941 and retired in 1981 as Master General of the Ordnance (Army Board Member for Procurement). He was Warden of St George's House, Windsor Castle from 1981 to 1986, and Director of the Council for Arms Control from 1986 to 1989. He writes and lectures on defence policy, arms control and ethical issues concerning peace and war. He is Vice-Chair of the Council on Christian Approaches to Defence and Disarmament and as co-editor of this book compiled the Technical Annex.

**David Fisher** was Deputy Head of the Defence and Overseas Secretariat in the Cabinet Office where he advised the Prime Minister on defence issues. Prior to that he was the Under Secretary in the Ministry of Defence responsible for defence equipment. He was Defence Counsellor in the UK Delegation to NATO where he helped revise Alliance defence policies and strategies following the end of the Cold War. He is currently Strategy Director of EDS. He regularly contributes to books and journals on defence and ethical issues and is the author of *Morality and the Bomb* (Croom Helm, 1985), a study of the ethics of nuclear deterrence written while he was a Research Fellow of Nuffield College, Oxford.

**Tim Garden** is the Liberal Democrat Defence spokesman in the House of Lords. He is a former nuclear bomber pilot, and the author of a book on nuclear strategy, *Can Deterrence Last?* (Buchan & Enright, 1984).

**Richard Harries** (Lord Harries of Pendregarth) was Bishop of Oxford since 1987. Before that he was Dean of King's College, London. He has published widely in the field of war and peace, in particular *Christianity and War in a Nuclear Age* (Mowbrays, 1986) and *Should a Christian Support Guerillas?* (Lutterworth, 1982). Most recently he chaired the working party of the House of Bishops, which produced *Countering Terrorism: Power, Violence and Democracy Post 9/11*. He has a number of doctorates and is a Fellow of the Royal Society of Literature. He is President of CCADD.

**Sir Michael Howard** is a Vice-President of CCADD and Life President of the International Institute for Strategic Studies. He founded the Department of War Studies at King's College London and was Professor of War Studies from 1963 to 1968. He became Chichele Professor of the History of War at Oxford, 1977–80, Regius Professor of Modern History at Oxford, 1980–89, and Professor of Military and Naval History at Yale, 1989–94. His many publications include *The Invention of Peace* (2000) and *The First World War* (2005). He was awarded the Order of Merit in 2005.

**Dr Peter Jarman** graduated in pure and applied nuclear physics, and then taught and did research in universities and research institutions in Britain, Australia, the USA and Switzerland before serving as the Europe Secretary of Quaker Peace and Service focusing on contacts with the peoples of the communist states of Europe. Subsequently he and his wife Roswitha served as Quaker representatives in Russia and on retirement he worked with the Swedish Transnational Foundation for Peace on post-war problems in the Balkans.

**Oliver Kamm** is a columnist for *The Times*, and the author of *Anti-Totalitarianism: The Left-Wing Case for a Neoconservative Foreign Policy* (Social Affairs Unit, 2005).

**Tony Kempster** DSc PhD MA is a retired scientist, now a peace activist, writer and singer with wide interests in ethics and education. He is General Secretary of the Anglican Pacifist Fellowship and Chair of the Movement for the Abolition of War. He is also a Director of the Peace Museum, Bradford, and a Management Committee member of the Council on Christian Approaches to Defence and Disarmament.

**Dr Julian Lewis** is the Shadow Defence Minister dealing with nuclear deterrence. Since 1997 he has been Conservative MP for New Forest East, and he served as a Deputy Director of the Conservative Research Department from 1990 to 1996. In the 1980s he was a leading campaigner against the CND. A second edition of his book *Changing Direction: British Military Planning for Post-war Strategic Defence, 1942–47* was published by Frank Cass in 2003.

**Michael MccGwire** is a former naval officer and NATO war-planner, with service in Moscow and in the Soviet naval section of the Defence Intelligence Staff. He has held the Strategic Studies chair at Dalhousie University, Canada, and was a Senior Fellow at the Brookings Institute DC from 1979 to 1990. He is an honorary Professor of International Politics at the University of Wales, Aberystwyth, and has written extensively on nuclear policy and deterrence for the last 20 years.

**Douglas Roche** has been special adviser on security and disarmament to the Holy See's UN delegation. He was Canadian Ambassador for Disarmament from 1984 to 1989 and in 1988 was Chair of the UN Disarmament Committee. He has won awards from the Mahatma Gandhi Foundation, and the Canadian Islamic Congress, and was a member of the Canadian Pugwash Group which won the Nobel Peace Prize in 1995. He is currently Chair of the Middle Powers Initiative. His most recent book is *Beyond Hiroshima* (Novalis, 2005).

**Dr Tom Sauer** is a lecturer in International Politics at the University of Antwerp and a post-Doctoral Research Fellow at the Institute for International and European Policy at the Katholieke Universiteit Leuven, Belgium. He is the author of *Nuclear Inertia: US Nuclear Policy After the Cold War* (I.B. Tauris, London, 2005).

**Roland Smith** was a member of the British Diplomatic Service from 1967 to 2002. He served for several years as Head of the Non-Proliferation Department, and from 1995 to 1998 was Director for International Security, with responsibility for all issues relating to defence and arms control. His last post was as Ambassador in Kiev.

**Brian Wicker** is Chair of the Council on Christian Approaches to Defence and Disarmament. He holds Master's degrees in English Literature, Philosophy and War Studies, and was Principal of Fircroft College of Adult Education in Birmingham from 1980 to 1988. He has been in opposition to nuclear weapons for nearly 50 years, and has contributed to several CCADD books dealing with just war and related topics. In 1985 the Catholic Truth Society published his *Nuclear Deterrence: What Does the Church Teach?*

# Foreword

# Michael Howard

Throughout the last half of the twentieth century the problem of nuclear weapons obsessed thinkers in the West. Moralists and strategists came together to agonize over the question, 'How could weapons of such total and indiscriminate destructiveness be used, or even credibly threatened, as "instruments of national policy" to fight or deter wars?' At each end of the spectrum of opinion there were absolutists who saw no problem. Some – admittedly not very many – saw them as weapons like any other. Others regarded them as an evil so great that their total abolition was a moral, especially a Christian, duty. But between lay a wide range of thinkers, civil and military, lay and ecclesiastical, who saw them as an existential problem that, however evil, could be neither wished away nor ignored, but had to be considered in all its complexity within the given framework of international relations, specifically the Cold War. This was the context in which the Council on Christian Approaches to Defence and Disarmament (CCADD) itself was founded, as a forum where Christians of all persuasions and professional backgrounds could come together and discuss the problem within the arena of their common beliefs.

With the end of the Cold War the problem lost its urgency, but it did not go away. Now a combination of circumstances has brought it to the fore again. The most alarming is a renewed polarization of the world, this time between an industrialized and modernizing 'West' and a resentful transnational community that sees itself exploited and marginalized and finds its voice in a militant Islamic movement whose extremists stop at nothing – certainly not their own self-destruction – to proclaim and prosyletize their own faith. Were such groups to obtain control of a state, and that state to acquire nuclear weapons, nuclear war might again become a terrifying possibility. Even for moderate governments the possession of such weapons could restore their perceived inferiority *vis-à-vis* what they see as a patronizing and dictatorial West. Under such circumstances, for how long would classical doctrines of deterrence formulated 50 years ago continue to be effective? But given the increased range, lethality and accuracy of conventional weapons, are nuclear arsenals any longer necessary?

It is in this context that the British government is now contemplating the renewal of an 'independent' nuclear deterrent that was acquired under totally different circumstances half a century ago. Do we still need it? Does it add anything to our own security or to global stability? Could the money not be better spent on improving the efficiency of our overstretched conventional forces? Would its abolition affect the attitudes or policies of any other States, nuclear or non-nuclear? In particular, how would it affect our relationship with the United States?

All these questions are no doubt being carefully considered in Whitehall, but they need to be far more widely and publicly debated. In this book CCADD has brought together the considered views of an impressive group of churchmen, politicians, military experts, civil servants, scientists, journalists, diplomats and peace activists. They cover the full range of opinion on the question and write with a moral seriousness and weight of expertise that makes it difficult to discount any of their arguments. Readers must weigh them and make up their own minds on what has once again become one of the most pressing problems of our age.

# Introduction

Before the next General Election Britain and the British government will be facing a momentous decision: whether to retain the UK's nuclear weapons for the long-term future, or to get rid of them completely once the current system is worn out. There is no third alternative, even if the decision can be postponed by prolonging the life of the current Trident system for a few more years.

The fundamental choice is stark: (a) If Britain decides to stick with its nuclear weapons for (say) the next 40 years (roughly the lifetime of the current Trident system), there seems little chance of any other state being willing instead to begin the process of unravelling the nuclear tangle. On the contrary, states which are at present undecided will be more strongly tempted to go nuclear for fear of becoming vulnerable to nuclear attack by their neighbours. The nuclear non-proliferation regime will then be in deadly peril. It would seem then that the world is doomed to suffer the nuclear nightmare for all the time ahead that anybody can foresee.

(b) On the other hand, if Britain were to go non-nuclear from around 2020, this would perhaps provide the only opportunity for the spiders' web in which much of the world is caught to be unravelled. The opportunities for political and economic progress, especially among the non-nuclear weapon states, would be immense.

Yet it would be far from certain that others would follow Britain's lead. The risk of a disarmed and isolated Britain would be real. Furthermore, it is sometimes argued, we would lose our place at the 'top table' of states, and thus our influence for good in the world. How valid are these objections? Both questions are dealt with at various points in the following pages.

It is already widely accepted that if Britain is to remain a nuclear weapons state, a decision to begin the process of replacing Trident with something else has to start soon. In this new century, is the United Kingdom prepared to take the bold plunge into nuclear disarmament, or will it decide to keep hold of the nuclear nurse for fear of finding something worse?

Today we in Britain face a wide-open window of political opportunity, but as Michael MccGwire points out, windows of opportunity are frequently spring-loaded to snap shut. Is this going to happen once again in the present case, or will the country do what needs to be done to ensure that the window stays open? People often say that it is impossible to get rid of nuclear weapons because they cannot be disinvented. True enough, but this argument fails to prove its point. After all, neither torture nor slavery can be disinvented: yet both of these evils have been outlawed by robust international laws and agreements, having first been abandoned by a few states (including Britain) acting on their own. Why should it not be possible to do the same with the threat of nuclear annihilation?

If this point has any validity, the process of nuclear elimination has to begin somewhere, and it is difficult to find a better place to begin it than in Britain. This is why the choice that lies before the United Kingdom is so momentous. And this is also why it is necessary for the British people, and their Members of Parliament, to think hard and long about it in public, before it is too late and wrong decisions are irrevocably made.

Hence the reason for this book, which attempts to put together the main elements of the necessary discussion. It presents views on both sides of the argument, and tries to present them fairly. The work has been sponsored by the The Council on Christian Approaches to Defence and Disarmament, which is a charity dedicated to promoting intelligent and fair-minded debate on justice and peace issues. But while the sponsoring body is of Christian provenance, the list of contributors is not confined to those who think of themselves as Christians. It is simply a gathering of people of varied experience, knowledge and background, who are well placed to put the arguments, for and against, in as clear and well-informed a way as possible.

At this point it seems appropriate to offer some guidance to the reader as to the contents of what follows. First of all, it will be helpful to point out things on which there is a consensus among the all contributors. After that it will be useful to indicate the main points on which there are clear differences of opinion. When this has been done the reader can better make up her or his own mind.

## Points of consensus

1 There can be no useful form of nuclear deterrence against terrorist gangs such as al-Qaeda. For deterrence depends for its effect on the rationality of the deterred party. This is why, for example, Khruschev calculated, during the Cuba crisis of 1962, that he would have to back off in order to avoid far worse harm befalling his country. Such a calculation would be unlikely to be made by a fanatical terrorist who is not afraid to blow himself up, along with his victims, for the cause he believes in. Furthermore, there is no way of knowing in advance what target a terrorist gang may try to hit. There was no way that a nuclear deterrent could have prevented the events of 9/11 from taking place.

2 There can be no nuclear deterrent based on sheer bluff. To maintain a credible deterrent, you have to be willing at some point (however remote) to *use* your nuclear weapons. It follows from this that nuclear deterrence depends on actual use of the weapon not being absolutely forbidden, either by law or ethics.

3 Majority public opinion in Britain favours the maintenance of nuclear weapons for the sake of national security. Hence

the 'disarmers' have a mountain of hostility to climb over. It also means that going for the retention of Britain's nuclear weapons would be a popular policy. (This may be part of the reason why the Blair government seems likely to go along with it, haunted as they are by the ghost of CND. Fear of losing the next General Election by adopting so unpopular a measure as unilateral nuclear disarmament must be a major factor in government calculations.)

4 The proliferation of nuclear weapons, beyond the states which already have them, is a dangerous possibility which ought to be resisted if at all possible. The Nuclear Non-Proliferation Treaty is therefore something that should be supported, and if possible strengthened, not weakened. (This is a point of consensus among virtually all shades of British opinion. It may not be so among the neo-con 'hawks' of the American administration.)

5 During the early years of the nuclear age, deterrence was unavoidably committed to attacking cities. This was because the inaccuracy of the delivery systems, and the huge size of the indiscriminate warheads, made hitting anything smaller than a city and its civilian population impossible (Hiroshima and Nagasaki for example). But this is no longer the case. Many modern deterrence-advocates make a case for a system of nuclear deterrence which is confined to 'legitimate', i.e. solely 'combatant' or 'counter-force' targets. (Whether their case stands up to rigorous analysis is another matter, and this is one of the crucial points of difference between the contributors to this book.)

6 Although not all contributors say so, it seems to be generally agreed that if Britain did not possess nuclear weapons already, we would not attempt to develop them, under the current conditions now that the Cold War is over. Furthermore, once our nuclear weapons have been eliminated from the state's armoury, most people seem to accept that there is virtually no chance of wanting to go back to the starting

point and begin all over again. So nuclear disarmament is an irrevocable 'once only' step.

7 The long-term future of international relations is extremely unpredictable, and nobody can be sure that there will not arise situations in the future when Britain is once more mortally threatened, either in its territory or its 'vital national interests', by a nuclear-armed state. This is the basis for the case made by retentionists that it is 'better to be safe than sorry', by hanging on to what we have already got. But, either way, risks have to be taken. So the question faced by both sides is: which is the better form of 'insurance policy' for Britain – the retention or the elimination of the destructive capacity of nuclear weapons?

8 It is clearly inconsistent for Britain to advocate measures to prevent other states from acquiring nuclear weapons while at the same time advocating retaining, and even modernizing them for itself. (But there is a difference, among the contributors to this book, as to the seriousness of this point. Some say it is simply an awkward problem that we can, must and should live with. Others say it is a source of grave injustice and hypocrisy, and indeed of a dangerous temptation by other resentful states to proliferate.)

9 While only Douglas Roche mentions it specifically, it seems clear that the Vatican 'now rejects nuclear deterrence completely in light of decisions by the US and other nuclear powers to make nuclear deterrence a permanent part of their defence policies'. This is a significant shift from the very limited tolerance of deterrence 'only as a temporary step on the road to nuclear disarmament', which Pope John Paul II offered in 1982 during the later stages of the Cold War.[1] The significance of this point is that the Holy See is a major Christian authority which, as a member of the UN, is nevertheless free to act on its own without the influence, on its proposals, of any national government policy.

So much for the points which contributors to this book accept. Now for the main bones of contention between them. These issues may be listed under the following heads: ethical, political, legal, technical/strategic and theological.

## Bones of Contention

### *Ethical issues*

1 Some contributors (e.g. Wicker and Roche) argue that nuclear deterrence is, of itself and unavoidably, murderous in character. That is to say, at some point the deterrer has to be willing to commit mass murder of the innocent if his deterrence is to 'work'. It follows from this that nuclear deterrence is intrinsically forbidden, because intentionally killing the innocent can *never* be just. Nuclear deterrence therefore cannot be supported by appeal to the criteria of 'just war', for this is concerned precisely with the *justice* of what is to be done in conflicts. For this reason, if for no other, it is imperative for Britain to give up its nuclear deterrent.

Other contributors however (e.g. Fisher, Harries) maintain that it is possible, with modern equipment, to mount a nuclear deterrent that can discriminate between civilians and 'combatants'. The latter include any of those involved in the political/military/industrial/technical activities of the deterred state. If this is done, a nuclear deterrent may be considered 'just' under the criteria of the just-war tradition. But it is to be noted at this point that where Fisher, for example, writes of the need to 'minimize' civilian casualties, Wicker insists on the much more stringent requirement that there be no intentional killing of the innocent ('innocent' here meaning, in accordance with its Latin sense, those who are not attempting to do the deterring side any harm). It is also to be noted that, whereas targeting policy is the crucial element in the retentionists' case, the disarmers deny this, pointing out that what matters is not the targets selected but the choice of what the deterrer wants his opponent to fear, for only this is a valid guide to the deterrer's intentions.

2 Embedded in the differences of view just mentioned is a difference about what the 'just-war' ethic underlying 'just deterrence' is about. Fisher, and also perhaps Kamm, Harries and Lewis, are 'principled consequentialists',[2] for whom the justice of deterrence depends on the balance of the good over the bad *consequences* which follow from its adoption, whereas Wicker insists that the 'classical' form of just-war thinking (and hence of just deterrence, if there can be such a thing) is rooted in the justice or otherwise of the *actions* involved in it. Furthermore, some contributors maintain that a rigorous ethic which categorically forbids nuclear deterrence is a necessary spur to the necessary radical reconstruction of international and global order, whereas a more 'accommodating' or permissive ethic leaves these affairs much as they are. This is a deep philosophical debate which it is not possible to enter into here, except to say that it stems from the convoluted history of ethics which has been inherited by the West.[3]

3 A further consideration arises with the argument put forward by Oliver Kamm that it is preferable to discuss the nuclear issue in political/strategic rather than ethical terms because the ethical case, whether for or against nuclear deterrence, is 'inconclusive'. If this only means that there is an unresolved disagreement about it, which cannot be bridged by those holding incompatible opinions, this is obvious to the point of being platitudinous. But it may mean something more substantial than this: namely that ethical judgements are of their very nature inconclusive because they do not deal in *truth* or *falsity*. In other words, ethical judgements are no more than personal opinions, based upon personal choices. For example, according to this view there can be no such thing as a form of action which is simply forbidden to human

beings (such as the intentional killing of the innocent) for there can be no such thing as a 'natural law' which forbids it. In this book, it would seem that Wicker and Roche (not to mention the Holy See), and perhaps also, from a different angle, David Fisher agree in holding that their ethical judgements are true and that therefore judgements incompatible with theirs are false. In this sense ethical judgements can well be conclusive even though many, perhaps most people refuse to accept them. Here is another point at which the discussion of the ethics of nuclear weapons touches the nerve of a deep philosophical question: a question which cannot be dismissed simply by voicing the opinion – for it may be no more than an opinion – that the issue is 'inconclusive'.

4 As has already been pointed out, a key difference between contributors concerns the ethical significance of targeting only 'counter-force' or 'combatant' elements in the enemy state. How far can or should we trust anybody's assurance that this targeting policy, adopted in advance for deterrent purposes, will 'stick' in the heat of a crisis? As Garden points out, with regard to the 'Negative Security Assurances' given by many nuclear states to those which do not possess nuclear weapons, such assurances 'won't be believed by an enemy in a crisis'.[4] Is not the same point valid also for any assurance that only counterforce targets will be chosen for deterrence purposes? For as we have seen, you cannot have a deterrent unless you are willing to use it. And in that case, is the deterrer's assurance that he won't strike non-combatants worth the paper it is written on?

5 Finally, under the ethical head, several contributors call nuclear deterrence an 'insurance' policy. Given that there is no course of action that is without risk, this seems a reasonable way of talking. But what sort of conditions would a nuclear deterrent 'insurance' policy require? Would it not entail something comparable to the following: a house is insured against burglary but on condition that it is equipped

in such a way that anybody entering it without permission would be immediately met with a dose of lethal poison gas and killed? Would any householder wish to pay for such a policy, with the possible risk of killing his own family?

## *Political issues*

1  Some contributors (e.g. Lewis) claim that the possession of a nuclear deterrent gives Britain its permanent seat at the UN Security Council, thus providing it with leverage in political negotiations which redound to its own security and that of other states. This is said to be a major 'plus' in its favour. But other contributors (Jarman, Harries, MccGwire) dispute this. They say there is no necessary connection between possession of nuclear weapons and permanent membership of the Security Council.

2  A related difference of view emerges over the question of Britain's influence over other states were she to renounce nuclear weapons for herself. MccGwire thinks that today Britain is 'uniquely qualified to initiate a process leading to the elimination of nuclear weapons', but retentionists are sceptical about this, believing that states are concerned to look after their own interests first and foremost.

3  MccGwire clearly differs from Lewis over the importance of the factors of inconsistency and resentment among the non-nuclear states over Britain's decision – if this is how we decide – to replace Trident with a new improved system while denying nuclear weapons to the 'have-nots', especially those like Iran who probably aspire to join the nuclear club. How far the resentment will turn into a resolve, by those states, to go nuclear come what may, despite the frowns of the nuclear-club members, cannot be fully known. But the contributors clearly differ over the importance to be attached to this consideration by comparison with the advantages supposedly gained by our retaining nuclear weapons for ourselves.

4 There is a related disagreement among the contributors as to the general impact, especially on disarmament and other peace-related efforts world-wide, of any British decision to renounce its nuclear weapons. Lewis and Kamm (and of course they are not alone – the Blair government probably agrees with them) think that the beneficial effect would be minimal. States look after their own interests pretty much without reference to what other states decide to do. Garden too sees some advantage in remaining nuclear-armed in foreign-policy terms: it gives Britain some leverage with the other nuclear weapons states, especially over the Nuclear Non-Proliferation Treaty. But, looking at things on a much larger canvas, MccGwire thinks differently. He clearly sees huge scope for Britain to take the lead, in a bigger partnership of non-nuclear states, over many of the most pressing issues of the day, especially those which are at present partly obscured or put to one side in the interests of keeping the nuclear club intact.

5 Garden, however, raises a question that the others tend to avoid. Why the hurry? he asks. It seems clear that in a purely technical sense, the current Trident system could be effectively prolonged well beyond its present 'sell-by' date. The world strategic scene might be a good deal clearer in a decade or so's time than it is now, so that Britain could then make a better-informed decision either way. It seems clear why the Blair government is in a hurry to make a decision: it wants the matter decided before the next General Election, and it wants it decided in favour of retention. But other voices are far from sure that this is wise, let alone ethically and politically advantageous. Of course, those who are against nuclear deterrence *tout court* and in principle do not think this point is of crucial importance. But politically it could be of very considerable force, especially when the economics of replacement are taken into account.

## Legal issues

The most obvious of these issues, over which there is a considerable divergence between Lewis and Smith, is what Britain is committed to under the Nuclear Non-Proliferation Treaty. Smith points to a number of constraints which the treaty lays upon its participants, notably in respect of the possible use of nuclear weapons against the use by others of chemical or biological weapons. Lewis however dismisses these as pretty insignificant. He also relegates the Article 6 commitment to nuclear disarmament negotiations to the harmless fairy-land of a mere 'aspiration'. He believes Britain has little or no need to take note of this, for the aspiration shows no sign of ever being fulfilled, and meanwhile Britain should look after its own interests, as any self-respecting sovereign state should. This difference comes out more clearly with the question of how far Article 6 constitutes a promise or moral obligation on the part of the participatory states, and especially the nuclear weapons states like Britain (as MccGwire insists), to begin negotiations for the complete elimination of nuclear weapons, as the International Court of Justice said in its judgement of 8 July 1996.

## Technical/strategic issues

1 For the purposes of this book, the only technical question that matters is how far the British deterrent is really 'independent'. Several of the retentionists make a good deal of the familiar claim that, in a crisis where the USA is not involved, Britain could 'go it alone' with her own independent nuclear weapons, rather as the French clearly could with theirs. But it is not clear that this is really so, although the key technical facts are kept secret so that outsiders cannot easily gain access to them. This is a major point, since it bears heavily upon the strategic case for retaining Britain's Trident. We

have therefore devoted a special Technical Annex to a discussion of this question, insofar as it is possible to do so without full access to secrets which those not 'in the know' are discouraged from finding out about. The Annex comes to two main conclusions. First, that if American technical and training support was withdrawn then British Trident would start to become obsolescent and inoperable in a matter of a year or two. Second, while the system remains in good shape, if the British Prime Minister were to order the submarine to fire in circumstances where America disapproved, then short of armed action against Britain there is probably nothing the President could do to stop it.

2  There is also a strategic issue as to whether nuclear deterrence depends on the *certainty* of response to threats (as Michael MccGwire and Julian Lewis insist) or on the preservation of *uncertainty* of response as David Fisher maintains. This is a long-standing debate in the context of deterrence theory, which has its implications for the ethical question of deterrent intentions, as Wicker suggests.

## Theological issues

Some theological thinking is presented in this book by Richard Harries. His thoughts about the meaning and implications of the Christian doctrine of the coming 'Kingdom of God', and its bearing on the ethical and other aspects of modern warfare, are put forward towards the end of his chapter. Since nobody else has dwelt on this point in the book there seems to be no 'bone of contention' over it, although it may be that different theological perspectives on the issues raised could have been discussed by some of the other contributors. Of course, the pacifist views outlined by Jarman and Kempster, not to mention the essentially negative judgement on nuclear weapons by the Vatican since the end of the Cold War, have their bearing on the theological questions underlying the book's purpose. The pacifist case clearly diverges from Richard Harries' 'just-war' presuppositions. But perhaps more surprisingly, an equally negative judgement has been arrived at by the Holy See, as Douglas Roche insists. The conclusion of this line of thinking is that there can be no such thing as a just way of deterring war, let alone of waging it, by the deployment of nuclear weapons.

The Holy See's radical post-Cold War position on this matter is too little discussed or understood by those involved in the wider debate, and is worth dwelling on in any collection of essays put together by a body that is concerned with Christian approaches to defence and disarmament.

Finally, the editors would like to thank all those who have volunteered, without any financial inducement, to provide the material necessary for the debate which this book is designed to stimulate. They alone have made it possible for CCADD to continue its tradition of publicizing security issues of major importance, by producing this book – and on time! All CCADD members are deeply indebted to them for their efforts.

*The Editors*

# 1  Should Trident be Replaced?

## RICHARD HARRIES

During the Cold War I supported, with some moral fear and spiritual trembling, a policy of nuclear deterrence by the NATO powers. I did this for three reasons. First, one hesitates to say that Soviet communism at the time was a unique evil, but it was certainly a very serious evil. It wasn't simply just another tyranny or regime in which there were severe human rights abuses. It wasn't that it was expansionist or even that it was atheistic. The reason was well brought out by the German theologian Helmut Thielicke who contrasted two chapters in the New Testament, Romans 13, in which Christians are enjoined to submit obediently to government, and Revelation 13, where the state has become demonic because it has usurped the function of God.[1] Thielicke argued that Soviet communism, like Nazi Germany, was no longer the state described in Romans 13 which was to be obeyed, but the state of Revelation 13 which had usurped the function of God and become demonic. It therefore had no more claim on us. It was a very serious evil – one that, in other terms, one might describe as based on the great lie. All tyrants and despots use lies from time to time, but lying was fundamental to Soviet communism because it was based on a false understanding of the nature of human beings and human society, in which the state functioned as God.

Second, I supported a policy of nuclear deterrence because I believed that it was essentially stable. Of course there was always the possibility of accident or miscalculation, but the Soviet authorities were rational. They calculated what was in

15

their interest, and for the first time in human history it could not conceivably have been in the interest of either the Soviet Union or NATO to have had a nuclear exchange. This had serious negative consequences, in the sense that under the nuclear umbrella all kinds of injustices had to be accepted, such as the invasion of Hungary and Czechoslovakia. But despite a great deal of scaremongering in some quarters (which had the useful effect of keeping before us the horrendous effects of a nuclear exchange) the system was fundamentally stable. There was a nuclear stalemate.

Third, I believed that there were some circumstances, however limited, in which the use of a nuclear weapon would be neither indiscriminate nor disproportionate.[2] Or to put it differently, I did not think that every possible use was essentially indiscriminate and disproportionate. Although there was always the possibility of escalation from a low-level exchange to one which was disproportionate and indiscriminate, the fear of escalation was one of the factors making for a stable deterrent system, and that possibility and fear could not be regarded as intrinsically immoral.

The world is very different now, as is the nature of the threat we face. There is no regime or threat comparable to Soviet communism. In short, Trident has absolutely no strategic use at the moment. This does not mean to say that nuclear weapons in some quarters are not a stabilizing factor. They are. It is difficult to avoid the conclusion that there would have been a terrible conventional war between India and Pakistan at the time of their latest stand-off, if it hadn't been apparent to both sides that their opponent had nuclear weapons and might use them. So in that situation the presence on both sides of nuclear weapons was probably a stabilizing factor which meant that overt conflict was avoided. It may also be that the presence of massive nuclear weapons by the United States is a sobering fact with which some countries, such as North Korea and Iran, seriously reckon.

The main threat facing us at the moment is a terrorist one.[3] The overall strategy against this should be based on the primacy of winning hearts and minds. The key weapon is good intelligence. If military force is used there will be a particular need for it to be both discriminate and proportionate because the terrorist group is likely to have lodged itself in a community. It's difficult to think of a scenario in which nuclear weapons would be used against a terrorist group.

There is always the possibility of a rogue regime, even one with evil intent. Here we have to make a distinction between a rogue regime which is in the grip of rulers who are totally reckless, who do not care whether the whole country is destroyed or not, and who are prepared to have the whole house destroyed around them Hitler fashion. Deterrence would have little effect on the minds of such rulers because rational calculation would not be the way they operated. It is possible of course that nuclear weapons might be used to eliminate the nuclear threat of such a regime, but that raises questions of proportion and discrimination, which are taken up later.

If the rogue regime operates on the basis of rational calculation, then they would indeed acknowledge, as did the Soviet Union during the Cold War, that there were no conceivable uses of nuclear weapons which could be regarded as in the interests of their state, if their enemy were prepared to retaliate in kind. So deterrence would indeed work. But this raises the question as to how evil that rogue regime is, whether it is an evil of the kind we faced with the Nazis and the Soviet Union, or whether it is just run-of-the-mill tyranny and despotism. If the latter, then the question is raised about whether the risks of actually having to use nuclear weapons would be justified, given the potential horrendous effects of such use.

In considering the question whether Trident should be replaced by a new, more advanced system, we are talking about Britain's nuclear role. For the foreseeable future the United States would continue to possess nuclear weapons and, if we believe that such possession is a stabilizing factor in a notoriously uncertain and volatile world, the existence of nuclear weapons in the hands of the United States would serve that stabilizing function. Britain would in fact shelter under her nuclear umbrella. What we have to imagine therefore is a situation in which that umbrella would no longer be available and Britain would be faced by a nuclear threat on its own, with the United States not prepared to offer any supporting counter threat. Some have suggested that this situation arose in relation to the Falklands conflict, when the United States would not have been prepared to deter Argentina if they had threatened to use nuclear weapons against Britain.

So there is a risk, however small, that at some point in the future the United Kingdom might be faced by a rogue regime offering a nuclear threat to our sovereignty or our essential interests. This regime, we assume, is capable of rational calculation and would be deterred if we possessed an independent deterrent. In this scenario the United States is not prepared to offer a counter threat. So there is a risk. But there are other kinds of risk that also have to be taken into the equation.

First, from a moral point of view, there is the continuing question as to whether in practice nuclear weapons could be used in such a way that they were both discriminate and proportionate. In theory the answer is yes, if the evil to be weighed against that risk is grave enough, as it was with the existence of the Soviet Union. But there is also the very severe risk that in actuality the use of nuclear weapons would be devastating in their effects on the civilian population and future generations.

The other aspect is the credibility of the Non-Proliferation Treaty and the political will to achieve further nuclear disarmament. The majority of nations in the world have been pressing for North Korea and Iran, for example, not to become nuclear weapons states. The United States in particular takes that possibility very seriously and is determined to oppose it. In response, there is the familiar cry of inconsistency, with Britain, among other nations, continuing to retain its nuclear weapons and claiming that they have a serious and legitimate defensive purpose: an argument, of course, that can be equally well used and has been equally well used by nations which don't, at the moment, possess nuclear weapons. The argument is sometimes put forward that if the United Kingdom divested itself of its nuclear weapons this would make absolutely no difference to the policy of nations that are thinking of acquiring them. But credibility is an important factor in achieving trusting relationships between potentially hostile nations. If Britain ceased to be a nuclear state this might not have very much effect on the thinking of the rulers of North Korea or Iran. But if it remains a nuclear state and continues to enhance its weapons system, there will continue to be the argument from such states, that there is a lack of consistency and therefore credibility in states who, while possessing nuclear weapons themselves, urge others not to do so.

From a strategic point of view, there is for the foreseeable future no serious threat to the United Kingdom from a nuclear weapons state, or a state that might conceivably obtain nuclear weapons. The main threat that the world faces is from terrorists, and nuclear weapons are not an appropriate or possible weapon to use against terrorist groups, who as likely as not will be embedded in civilian populations. There is a just conceivable theoretical threat in the future, on the basis that the United Kingdom is decoupled for defensive purposes from the United States and it faces a nation that has nuclear weapons whose regime operates on the basis of rational calculation, and which wishes to threaten our fundamental interests. The government of the United Kingdom is right to think about such possibilities. It is charged with the responsibility of protecting its citizens and it needs to take every possible scenario into account. We do indeed live in a notoriously uncertain and volatile world in which evil forces are likely to erupt in unpredictable ways, and it is folly to project a safe future on the basis of present strategic calculations. Yet there are some risks which, perhaps, ought to be taken, even by governments. We do not live in a risk-free world. At this point a Christian will look for a New Testament perspective.

Christians in the New Testament were conscious of living between the times, between the time of Christ's resurrection and his coming again in glory.[4] During this interim period, in which we still live, it is necessary for human institutions, such as the state and government, to continue, because there can be no viable or meaningful human life without some degree of order, both nationally and internationally, and in a fallen world this depends on a degree of coercion. So long as God wills human life to continue, he wills those human institutions to continue. Yet they will come to an end, as will all human coercion. Christ is risen and within him we have a promise and pledge of a new world which operates on the basis of persuasive love alone. Christians have resolved the tension between what is necessary to survive now and that ultimate state of affairs brought into existence by Jesus in various ways. I believe that it is a mistake to dissolve the tension, either by assuming that the Kingdom of God can be acted out in its fullness here and now, without any kind of qualification of compromise, which leads to principled pacifism, or to the idea that the ethic of the Kingdom has no bearing upon present power realities. Present power realities have to be taken into account, we need government and we need sometimes to use force in the international sphere. But the ethic of the Kingdom bears upon these realities and we should look for and work for signs and anticipations of what will one day be here in its totality and perfection. This has a bearing on how we weight different kinds of risk.

There is another factor derived from the New Testament, namely that we are to 'fear not'. Human life will never be risk-free and we cannot anticipate and guard against every possible kind of risk. The attempt to do so, to make ourselves or our nation absolutely secure and invulnerable, is hubristic folly. So the word of the Lord comes: 'fear not'.[5] This should not be taken as an excuse to be reckless. We are also bidden to be prudent, to count the cost, to be responsible. But this is very different from thinking that every kind of risk can be managed. So there are occasions when a Christian, without being irresponsible, will want to act on the basis of trust and good will, even in a world where there is still malicious mistrust and ill will. And though it might be argued that an individual Christian could be justified in acting in this way when it is only his or her own interests at stake, governments have a responsibility to act for the country as a whole and all its citizens, and are never justified in taking any such risk. But the ethic of the Kingdom of God is not just for Christians, it bears upon the whole of human existence and all people, whether they are believers or not. Governments themselves can give a moral lead, as the United Kingdom has sought to do over issues such as debt relief for the poorest countries in the world, overseas aid and trade justice. No doubt politicians who are committed to such causes will argue that they are in Britain's best long-term interests – and so they might be. Nevertheless, the moral passion behind such causes is one that goes beyond prudential calculations about what is in the national interest.

So we are talking about risk and what risks it would be right to take. In a world of notorious uncertainty, with the possibility of an as yet unknown threat arising, a prudent government will argue in favour of replacing Trident, for we simply don't know what the future holds. A Christian can argue, first, that we can never make ourselves absolutely secure and safe, and the attempt to do so is misconceived. There are risks whatever decision is made. Second, one kind of risk, which is not always considered, is the moral risk of actually having to use nuclear weapons in a way that would be indiscriminate and disproportionate.

Third, if we believe in non-proliferation, the credibility of nuclear weapons states is a major factor in both the strategic and moral equation. Fourth, without being reckless, if there is a balance of risks to be struck, not just the individual Christians but a government may be right on occasions to act on the assumption that trust, rather than mistrust, good will rather than ill will, persuasion rather than coercion, are the values of the Kingdom which will ultimately prevail and therefore can be anticipated in some way, in however fragmentary and partial a fashion, even here and now.

# 2  Disarmament Versus Peace

## JULIAN LEWIS

### Certainty and deterrence

In the closing stages of the Second World War, a series of terrible blows rained down on the Japanese homeland. City after city was attacked and civilian casualties were measured in the tens of thousands. Still, the Japanese did not surrender – any more than did the Germans, under a similar weight of bombardment, until overrun by the Allied armies.

When the atomic bombs were used against two more Japanese cities, however, the shock effect on the country's rulers was decisive, even though initially the numbers of casualties were no greater than those inflicted by the conventional attacks against Tokyo and elsewhere. In my view, the real change brought by the atomic bomb was not the scale of the destruction it could inflict, but the *absolute certainty* that that destruction would be inflicted and could not be avoided.

The 'fog of war' is a phrase much beloved by military historians. Not only has war traditionally been a confusing process, it has generally amounted to a massive gamble. The record of Hitler's career is of a succession of greater and greater gambles, culminating in his disastrous decision to invade the Soviet Union in 1941. Later that year, Imperial Japan similarly gambled against enormous odds in deciding to attack the American Fleet at Pearl Harbor. Conceivably, some acts of historical aggression like these might still have been undertaken if their perpetrators had known in advance that they were absolutely certain eventually to be defeated – but this is very much to be doubted.

Gamblers may often risk incurring a devastating defeat, but only because they see a significant possibility of victory against the odds.

When the thousand-bomber raids were launched against German and Japanese cities, a whole variety of possible outcomes might have resulted. At one end of the spectrum, the mass bomber formations might have achieved their aim, destroyed their target and returned to base with very few losses of their own. At the other end of the spectrum, the bombers might have been intercepted and attacked, diverted from their target, which remained unscathed, and forced to suffer very heavy losses themselves, as happened in the infamous Nuremberg raid.

There was no real way of knowing in advance how such encounters would work out – until, that is, the coming of the atomic bomb. At the risk of seeming fanciful, let us imagine that the Germans and the Japanese had known in advance that their potential victims, the democracies, would develop nuclear weapons before the end of the wars they were about to unleash. Is it likely that they would have proceeded to do so in the certain knowledge that their principal cities were absolutely certain to be obliterated? Those of us who subscribe to the doctrine of deterrence believe that even the most reckless dictators would hesitate to act in the face of inevitable retaliatory destruction. Indeed, the theory had already been formulated before the atomic bomb had even been tested.

In a top secret report for the Chiefs of Staff in June 1945, Professor Sir Henry Tizard wrote that the only answer which he and other senior defence scientists could see to the atomic bomb was to be prepared to use it in retaliation:

A knowledge that we were prepared, in the last resort, to do this might well deter an aggressive nation. Duelling was a recognised method of settling quarrels between men of high social standing so long as the duellists stood twenty paces apart and fired at each other with pistols of a primitive type.

If the rule had been that they should stand a yard apart with pistols at each other's hearts, we doubt whether it would long have remained a recognised method of settling affairs of honour.[1]

This argument was only the latest in a long line of similarly hard-headed but hopeful views. The motto: 'If you desire peace, be prepared for war' was essentially the same, as was the statement in the early days of aviation: 'When German bombers can destroy London and British bombers can destroy Berlin, Germany and Britain will never again go to war.' Nor is it realized by the world at large that Alfred Nobel – of Peace Prize fame – was actually the inventor of dynamite. He felt that, such was the destructive power of this new explosive, war would become too costly for countries to contemplate.

Why the Tizard scenario of peace through mutually assured destruction stood the test of time better than the earlier arguments was the factor of certainty (or 'assuredness') which atomic weapons for the first time guaranteed. Earlier explosives, like dynamite, and earlier means of delivery, like manned bombers, still left the outcome of the encounter in doubt. Even where both sides were similarly armed, there remained enough of a chance that one of them would suffer total defeat while the other enjoyed total victory, to make the gamble of waging war seem worthwhile. There was, in short, too much uncertainty as to what the outcome would be.

## Morality and deterrence

The dawning of the atomic age was thus accompanied by what seemed to be an extreme ethical paradox: peace could apparently best be maintained by the possession of, and the threat to use, weapons which could obliterate tens of thousands of people in an instant.

Simply because nuclear weapons, *if used,* would cause hideous destruction and loss of life, it has often been argued that there is something immoral in their very possession. Yet, no weapon is moral or immoral in itself. Ethics enter the equation only when one considers the motivation for possessing weapons and the uses to which they are put.

If the consequence of possessing a lethal weapon is that nobody uses lethal weapons, while the consequence of not possessing a lethal weapon is that someone else uses his lethal weapons against you, which is the more moral thing to do: to possess the weapons and avoid anyone being attacked, or to renounce them and lay yourself open to aggression? I have no doubt about the answer, and neither has a consistent majority of British public opinion.

Twenty-five years ago, when working professionally against the campaign for British unilateral nuclear disarmament, I began commissioning professional polling firms to ask the following question: 'Do you think that Britain should continue to possess nuclear weapons as long as other countries have them?' Year after year the result showed a remarkable consistency – two-thirds of the British people thought we should keep them under these circumstances and one-quarter thought that we should renounce them unconditionally. These proportions did not change even after the end of the Cold War, and I doubt if they have greatly changed today.

If possession of nuclear weapons is inherently unethical, it is surprising (to put it mildly) that a large majority of civilized British citizens should time and again endorse it. Without wishing to be presumptuous, I suggest that the reason for their doing so is the accurate belief that it is both sensible and ethical to hold on to these weapons in a dangerous world, if the most likely outcome is a decrease rather than an increase in the probability of war breaking out.

The central problem which has to be faced by those who argue that the mere possession of, or the threat to use, nuclear weapons in retaliation is morally unacceptable, is the extreme level of destructiveness which conventional warfare had reached before the atomic bomb was invented. If it is the case that possessing a deadly weapon or being willing to threaten to use it in retaliation will avert a conflict in which millions would otherwise die, can it seriously be claimed that the more ethical policy is to renounce the weapon and let the millions meet their fate? Even if one argues that the threat to retaliate is itself immoral, is it as immoral as the failure to forestall so many preventable casualties?

This is, in reality, a variation on the argument against absolute pacifism which the late Leonard Cheshire VC illustrated when such issues were being debated 20 years ago. He set out the scenario of a security guard who is the only person in a position to prevent a terrorist from opening fire on a queue of passengers in an airport lounge. According to most people's values, not only is it morally correct for him to shoot the armed terrorist, it would be profoundly unethical for him to decline to do so. This is without prejudice to the fact that the security guard might well be right to feel that it was a tragedy that he had to take anyone's life at all. Moral choices are, as often as not, choices to determine the lesser of two evils. In the case of possessing and threatening to use a horrifying weapon, or renouncing it with the result that such weapons are actually used against one's own society, only the purest pacifist can be in any doubt about preferring the former.

## Changing times and changing threats

Many of the people who oppose Britain's retention and replacement of nuclear weapons in the twenty-first century also advocated unilateral nuclear disarmament, despite the level of the Soviet threat, during the Cold War. There are, however, significant numbers who believe that what was necessary then no longer applies now. This brings us to the central problem of *predictability*.

From time to time wars break out in circumstances which were anticipated; but, more often than not, they arise totally unexpectedly. The Yom Kippur War in 1973 took even hyper-sensitive Israel by surprise. The Falklands War, nine years later, took Britain by surprise. The invasion of Kuwait in 1990 took everyone by surprise. And the attacks on 11 September 2001 took the world's only superpower by surprise. There was nothing new in any of this – as a detour into the archives strikingly illustrates: from August 1919 until November 1933 British foreign and defence policy was hamstrung by a prediction that the country would not be engaged in a war with another major power for at least a decade. This had a dangerously adverse effect on necessary rearmament when the international scene darkened. Arguing against the continuation of this so-called 'Ten Year Rule' in January 1931 when Secretary of the Committee of Imperial Defence, Sir Maurice Hankey, observed:

> As a nation we have been prone in the past to assume that the international outlook is in accordance with our desires rather than with the facts of the situation . . . We are also apt to forget how suddenly war breaks out. In 1870, a fortnight before the event, we were not in the least expecting the outbreak of the Franco–Prussian War. The same was true in 1914. A fortnight after the murder of the Austrian Archduke, a debate took place in the House of Commons on foreign affairs. The European situation was hardly referred to at all. More attention was given to the preparations for the next Peace Conference! . . . There was no statement made on the subject of the European crisis in Parliament until July 27 . . . We really had, at the outside, not more than ten days' warning . . . How foolish a Government would have looked that had reaffirmed an assumption of ten years of peace during the early part of 1914![2]

The lesson of history is that onset of armed conflicts is inherently unpredictable. This is why it makes sense to keep in being an army, a navy and an air force during long periods of peace. The same applies *a fortiori* to the nuclear deterrent. Investment in armed forces in apparently peaceful times is analogous to the payment of premiums on insurance policies. No one knows when the accident or disaster may happen against which one is insuring: if one did, one could probably avoid it and save oneself the cost of the premiums! It is rare indeed, in terms of international politics, that one can rule out the recurrence of a major military threat from every quarter just because it has receded from a particular potential enemy.

With the benefit of hindsight, the Second World War is often regarded as a disaster predetermined by mistakes made at the end of the First World War. Yet, in the 1920s, there was so little sign of an obvious enemy that each of Britain's three Armed Services prepared its hypothetical contingency plans against an entirely different theoretical foe: the Navy against Japan, the Army against Russia, and the RAF against France! In those days, the choice of possible enemy would seriously affect the nature of the defence policy designed to meet the threat. Fortunately, the British strategic nuclear deterrent is less dependent than conventional armed forces upon the correct identification of the enemy in advance. Any country which emerges as a potential aggressor with mass-destruction weapons, in the next three or four decades, will be vulnerable to retaliation from Trident or its successor. And this is the sort of time scale which we have to consider.

Each generation of the strategic nuclear deterrent functions for a period of 30 years or more. The actual replacement of the Trident system, if it occurs, will not even begin for at least another 15 years. No one can possibly foretell what dangers will face us between the years 2020 and 2050, just as the threats facing us today would have seemed bizarre to politicians and military planners at the height of the Cold War in the 1980s. During periods of peace, democratic states naturally tend to scale down their conventional fighting services, but they try to do so in a way which is reversible should the international scene darken. This option does not apply to the nuclear deterrent, which has always been set at the minimum level regarded as essential for credibility. Just as it makes sense to keep minimum conventional forces in being as an insurance policy against unpredictable future conventional threats, the same applies all the more strongly to a minimum strategic nuclear deterrent. There can be no more assurance that a nuclear or major chemical or biological threat will not arise in the next half-century than that major land, sea or air threats will not have to be faced. If it is right to insure against the latter, it is essential to insure against the former.

## After the Cold War

Apart from those who have always opposed British nuclear weapons, irrespective of the level of threat, some politicians, some churchmen and commentators, and even some military figures who used to support it, have now changed their minds. This is primarily because the Cold War is over, America appears to be the dominant world power, and the principal threats today emanate from rogue regimes and stateless terrorist groups. Let us consider each of these in turn.

First, the ending of the Cold War removes the danger of nuclear confrontation with Russia for as long as that country continues to tread, however hesitantly, the democratic road. Indeed, it is striking to note that many prophets of nuclear doom during the 1970s and 1980s have been all but silenced by the change in East–West relations, even though enough nuclear weapons remain in US and Russian hands to destroy the world's main population centres with many warheads to spare. This illustrates the fact that *it is not the weapons themselves which we have to fear but the nature of the governments that possess them*. As soon as Russia turned away from totalitarianism, the main concern about her nuclear arsenal shifted from those devices under the control of the Kremlin to those which might leach out from Russian stockpiles and fall into the hands of other regimes which remained more hostile.

One concept which advocates of nuclear disarmament have traditionally ignored is the propensity for dictatorships to go to war with dictatorships, and for democracies and dictatorships to clash, while few – if any – examples exist of democracies attacking each other. This suggests that it is quite right to have fewer qualms about the possession of deadly weapons by democracies, though regarding their possession by dictatorships as wholly unacceptable. There is no comparison between the two, and it is a constant failing of the disarmament lobby to try to project values of reasonableness, tolerance, goodwill and peaceful intent onto states under the control of despots, fanatics and dictators.

The ending of the Cold War rightly caused a reduction in international tension; but the impossibility of predicting the emergence of future conventional and nuclear threats means that the permanent dismantling of our nuclear deterrent cannot possibly be anything other than a reckless gamble.

Second, the current period of America's solo superpower status in no way diminishes the case for an independent British deterrent. Nuclear weapons, by their very nature, have devastating potential even in very small numbers. Quite apart from the prospect of unpredictable major threats in the longer term, the current enmity towards Britain by near-nuclear regimes like Iran suggests that unilateralism would be fraught with danger. It used to be pointed out that the British Polaris fleet had done nothing to deter Argentina from invading the Falkland Islands. Certainly, there was never a prospect of democratic Britain threatening to use its ultimate weapon except in response to a mortal threat against the cities of the United Kingdom. What would have been the case, though, if the Argentine junta had possessed even a few atomic weapons or other mass-destruction devices? Without a nuclear force of her own, would Britain have dared to respond conventionally to the occupation of the Islands by a nuclear-armed military junta?

Time and again the United Kingdom and the United States have stood side by side in international conflicts. If this pattern continues, the prospect could arise of a nuclear-armed enemy regarding it as safer to threaten or attack the smaller of the two Allies. The danger would then arise of a possible miscalculation by an aggressor thinking that the US would not respond in kind to an attack with mass-destruction weapons on British cities. If this were a miscalculation, the attacker would discover it only when it was too late, instead of having been deterred at the outset by the knowledge that Britain could respond in kind on her own behalf.

These considerations clearly bear on the third issue – that of rogue regimes. Several of them are already nuclear powers or on the verge of becoming so. The notion that they will abandon such a course indefinitely in response to unilateral British nuclear disarmament is totally unrealistic. Those who subscribe to it continually make the error of projecting civilized values onto extremist governments who hold them totally in contempt.

Turning, fourth, to the current emergence of non-state terrorist groups, it is absolutely correct that strategic nuclear weapons are of no relevance whatsoever. Neither are aircraft carriers, main battle tanks, guided-missile destroyers or any other heavyweight military equipment. The presence of a serious terrorist threat is clearly an argument in favour of expanded counter-insurgency forces and security and intelligence services. It is no argument at all for the abolition of those military capabilities which are designed to meet other types of threat which this country has faced in the past and may well face again in the future.

## Nuclear proliferation

Does proliferation make Britain's continued possession of nuclear weapons unethical? There might be a case for arguing this if it could be shown that there were a causal link between our continued possession of a strategic nuclear deterrent and the decision of one or more named countries to acquire nuclear weapons. During the Cold War era, the proliferation argument was often used by one-sided nuclear disarmers in their campaign against Polaris, Trident and the deployment of cruise missiles. Yet, whenever asked to *name* a specific nuclear or near-nuclear country which would be likely to abandon its nuclear ambitions if we unilaterally renounced ours, the CND and its fellow-travellers were notably unforthcoming. Countries make the decision whether or not to seek to acquire mass-destruction weapons according to hard-headed calculations of their own strategic interests. A quixotic renunciation by democratic Britain is not very likely to encourage any undemocratic state to follow suit. On the contrary, it is more likely to encourage any such state which views Britain as a potential enemy to redouble its efforts to join the WMD club, given that we would no longer have the means to threaten retaliation against nuclear, biological or chemical aggression.

What does the Non-Proliferation Treaty actually commit the United Kingdom to do? Article VI of the NPT is often referred to, but seldom quoted in full. This is what it states:

Each of the Parties to the Treaty undertakes to pursue negotiations in good faith on effective measures relating to cessation of the nuclear arms race at an early date and to nuclear disarmament, and on a Treaty on general and complete disarmament under strict and effective international control.

There are thus three obligations, only the first of which is time-limited. This is to end 'the nuclear arms race' at 'an early date'. Given that the United Kingdom – and, for that matter, France and China – have never engaged in a nuclear arms race, their policy of each having a minimum strategic nuclear deterrent does not fall foul of this provision. None of these countries has ever sought to match the nuclear stockpiles of Russia or the United States. Each has been content to possess a much smaller nuclear capability, provided that it is adequate to threaten an unacceptable level of retaliation if attacked. The same would apply to any replacement system for Trident.

It is true that Article VI aspires to both 'nuclear disarmament' and 'a Treaty on general and complete disarmament' as well – but this is nothing more than an aspiration for the indefinite future. What it amounts to is nothing less than a world completely disarmed of all weapons of every description 'under strict and effective international control'. This utopia would require several things to happen: the creation of a World Government; the establishment of foolproof methods of preventing clandestine rearmament; and, above all, a revolution in the minds of people so that warfare became redundant. As my Parliamentary colleague, Shadow Defence Secretary Liam Fox, has aptly observed:

> Nothing in the Article requires worldwide nuclear disarmament to be achieved prior to worldwide conventional disarmament. This is just as well: to abolish all nuclear weapons in a world left bristling with all sorts of other deadly armaments would be to make the world safe again for the disastrous conflagrations which killed millions between 1914 and 1918 and between 1939 and 1945.

## Conclusion

During the inter-war years, the process of disarmament was taken to new heights of complexity, but it achieved only this: the peace-loving democracies disarmed each other and themselves, while the rogues, the villains, the bandits, the dictators and the tyrants re-armed in secret, threatened democracy and destroyed the peace of the world. After the final defeat of the Nazis, the democratic states faced a new challenge and a variation on an old dilemma. The challenge was that of confrontation with Soviet communism, the dilemma was whether to try to defuse it by disarmament or to contain it by deterrence.

The fact that the Third World War did not break out is not, of itself, conclusive proof that containment by deterrence was successful. It is of the nature of deterrence that, whenever it works, its opponents can always argue that the war would not have happened in any case. Yet, the fact that there were so many small but deadly wars fought between client states of the superpowers (but not between the superpowers themselves) strongly suggests that the mutual threat of nuclear annihilation had something to do with the restraint exercised by the superpowers themselves.

This essay will not make pleasant reading for decent, civilized and pious practitioners of the Christian Faith. The implications of my argument are not designed to cater for well-intentioned democrats who desire only the best for their own people and who project their decency upon other states and societies. But the bloody history of the twentieth century – not to mention all the wars of antiquity – amply illustrates the depths of evil and malevolence which some ideologues and megalomaniacs are willing to plumb. As Dean Inge sadly concluded: 'it takes in reality only one to make a quarrel. It is useless for the sheep to pass resolutions in favour of vegetarianism whilst the wolf remains of a different opinion.' The purpose of the British nuclear deterrent remains what it has always been: to minimize the dreadful prospect of the United Kingdom being attacked by mass-destruction weapons. It is not a panacea and it is not designed to deter every type of threat. Nevertheless, the threat which it is designed to counter is so overwhelming that no other form of military capability could manage to prevent it. The possession of the deterrent may be unpleasant, but it is an unpleasant necessity the purpose of which lies not in its actual use but in its nature as the ultimate 'stalemate weapon'. And, in the nuclear age, stalemate is the most reliable source of security available to us all.

# 3  Nuclear Weapons and Morality: An Unequivocal Position

## DOUGLAS ROCHE

When the first atomic bombs destroyed Hiroshima and Naga-saki in 1945, it could hardly have been imagined that 60 years later more than 30,000 nuclear weapons would be in existence. The Cold War is long over, but half the world population still lives under governments brandishing nuclear weapons. More than $12 trillion has so far been spent on these instruments of mass murder, which is a theft from the poorest people in the world. The present nuclear weapons crisis has, in fact, led to the opening of the Second Nuclear Age.

First, we must understand the dimensions of the crisis. The long-standing nuclear weapons states – the United States, Russia, the United Kingdom, France and China – are making nuclear weapons permanent instruments of their military doctrines. India, Pakistan and Israel have joined the 'nuclear club'. North Korea has tried to get into it. Iran is suspected of trying to acquire the capacity to convert nuclear fuels for peaceful purposes into nuclear weapons. NATO is maintaining American nuclear weapons on the soil of six European countries, and the US is preparing 'reliable replacement' warheads with new military capabilities.

The US and Russia have put new emphasis on the warfighting role of nuclear weapons. The nuclear weapons states refuse to give up their nuclear arsenals, and feign surprise that other nations, seeing that nuclear weapons have become the currency of power in the modern world, are trying to acquire them. So are terrorists. No major city in the world is safe from the threat of a nuclear attack. The risk of accidents is multiplying daily. All these are the characteristics of the Second Nuclear Age.

Thinking that the nuclear weapons problem went away with the end of the Cold War, much of the public is oblivious to the new nuclear dangers. UN Secretary-General Kofi Annan is trying to warn governments and the public, but few are listening. In the case of many politicians, they don't even know that they *don't* know about this greatest threat to human security the world has ever faced. They do not recognize the continued existence of enormous stocks of nuclear weapons, most with a destructive power many times greater than the atomic bomb that destroyed Hiroshima and Nagasaki.

Nuclear weapons are instruments of pure evil. A nuclear explosion, either by design or accident, would kill massive numbers of people, create international chaos, and cripple the world economy.

Nuclear weapons are devoid of the slightest shred of moral legitimacy. Prominent jurists consider their use illegal in any possible circumstance. The nuclear weapons states are deliberately undermining the rule of law in maintaining them.

It staggers the imagination to consider what the enormous sums spent on nuclear weapons could have done for education, health and other requisites for the development of peoples everywhere. The United States spends $110 million *every day* on the maintenance of its nuclear forces and seeking money from Congress for new ones. This is driving world military spending, which exceeded $1 trillion in 2004, a 20 per cent increase in two years.

Governments have thrown democracy out of the window in their zeal for armaments. Nowhere have citizens clamoured for nuclear weapons. Rather, governments have either imposed them or manipulated public opinion to get people to quietly accept them. A 2002 poll of citizens in 11 countries, including the US and Canada, showed that 86 per cent of people either strongly agree (72 per cent) or agree to some extent (14 per cent) that all nations should sign a treaty to ban all nuclear weapons. Governments are ignoring this opinion; the public, except for core groups of activists, is not actively demanding that governments move toward such a treaty. Instead, the public is saying, we should cure the worst of poverty and restore the environment.

In this new nuclear age, when public attention is sapped by the repercussions of the terrorist attacks of 11 September 2001, including terrorist attacks on the mass transit systems of Madrid and London, the entire framework of nuclear disarmament is in danger of being swept away. The month-long 2005 Review Conference of the Non-Proliferation Treaty ended in deadlock between the nuclear haves and have-nots.

This deadlock is so severe that the document issued by world leaders at the Summit marking the 60th anniversary of the United Nations was shorn of any reference to disarmament and non-proliferation because of the obstinacy of a very small number of states.

Meanwhile, the Comprehensive Nuclear Test Ban Treaty is stagnating. Strategic arms reductions between the US and Russia, which together possess 96 per cent of all nuclear weapons, is atrophying. The ongoing work of the Conference on Disarmament in Geneva is paralyzed. An effort by some countries at the UN Disarmament Committee in 2005 to kick-start negotiations was scuttled, again by a powerful few.

Time is running out. The Pugwash Conferences on Science and World Affairs, which won the 1995 Nobel Peace Prize for its work on nuclear disarmament, has noted:

The difficulties and even the possibility of a collapse of the nuclear non-proliferation regime, the weakening of the taboos in place since 1945 on the use of nuclear weapons, coupled with the dangers of a terrorist group detonating a nuclear explosive device, combine to produce a recipe for unmitigated disaster.

Though the voice of religion has been raised against nuclear weapons, the volume of that voice needs to be turned up in the light of the developments of the Second Nuclear Age. The religions of the world need to proclaim that nuclear weapons and human security cannot co-exist.

Definitive Catholic teaching on nuclear deterrence is found in Vatican II and subsequent statements by Pope John Paul II. Vatican Council II taught:

Any act of war aimed indiscriminately at the destruction of entire cities or of extensive areas along with their population is a crime against God and man himself. It merits unequivocal and unhesitating condemnation.[1] (Pastoral Constitution on the Church in the Modern World, No. 80)

The Catechism of the Catholic Church, published in 1992 on the 30th anniversary of the opening of the Vatican Council, affirmed the permanent validity of the moral law during armed conflict. It stated, 'The mere fact that war has regrettably broken out does not mean that everything becomes licit between the warring parties.' It warns against modern warfare with the opportunity it provides to commit crimes against God and humans through the use of atomic, biological and chemical weapons. The *Catechism* also draws attention to 'rigorous consideration' that must be given to claims of legitimate defence, stating: 'The use of arms must not produce evils and disorders graver than the evil to be eliminated. The power of modern means of destruction weighs very heavily in evaluating this condition.'

Though they elaborated their concern that a universal public authority be put in place to outlaw war, the Fathers of Vatican

II rather grudgingly accepted the strategy of nuclear deterrence. The accumulation of arms, they said, serves 'as a deterrent to possible enemy attack'. Thus 'peace of a sort' is maintained, though the balance resulting from the arms race threatens to lead to war, not eliminate it. Pope John Paul II restated the Catholic position on nuclear deterrence in a message to the UN Second Special Session on Disarmament in 1982:

> In current conditions, 'deterrence' based on balance, certainly not as an end in itself but as a step on the way towards a progressive disarmament, may still be judged morally acceptable. Nonetheless, in order to ensure peace, it is indispensable not to be satisfied with the minimum, which is always susceptible to the real danger of explosion.

In this statement, it is readily seen that deterrence, in order to be acceptable, must lead to disarmament measures. Consequently, deterrence as a single, permanent policy is not acceptable. The American Bishops' 1983 Pastoral Letter on War and Peace took up this theme. Though the bishops expressed a strong 'No' to nuclear war, declaring that a nuclear response to a conventional attack is 'morally unjustifiable', and were sceptical that any nuclear war could avoid the massive killing of civilians, the bishops gave a 'strictly conditioned moral acceptance of nuclear deterrence'.

In a five-year follow-up to their letter, the bishops set out criteria to be met in order to continue this morally justifiable basis for deterrence. For example, the bishops said that, in order to be acceptable, nuclear deterrence could not be based on the direct targeting of urban populations. Also, the bishops opposed weapons combining size, accuracy and multiple warheads in a credible first-strike posture. A subsequent follow-up in 1993, 'The Harvest of Justice is Sown in Peace', repeated that 'nuclear deterrence may be justified only as a step on the way toward progressive disarmament'. The bishops held that 'security lies in the abolition of nuclear weapons and the strengthening of international law'.

As the 1990s progressed, it became clear that US policy was not moving to nuclear disarmament. Even before the arrival of the Bush administration in 2001, the US rejected a no-first-use policy and adopted flexible targeting strategies to use nuclear weapons either pre-emptively or in response to chemical and biological weapon attacks. The Bush administration's Nuclear Posture Review explicated the maintenance of nuclear weapons for war-fighting strategies.

In 1998, seeing the institutionalization of nuclear deterrence taking place, 75 US Catholic bishops signed a statement criticizing the US for moving beyond original nuclear deterrence policies 'to which we grudgingly gave our moral approval in 1983'. The bishops said they were painfully aware that many policy-makers sincerely believe that possessing nuclear weapons is vital for national security. 'We are convinced, though, that it is not. Instead, they make the world a more dangerous place.'

> We cannot delay any longer. Nuclear deterrence as a national policy must be condemned as morally abhorrent because it is the excuse and justification for the continued possession and further development of these horrendous weapons.

In 1997, the Holy See's Permanent Representative at the United Nations, Archbishop Renato Martino, was moving in the same direction when he told the UN Committee on Disarmament:

> Nuclear weapons are incompatible with the peace we seek for the 21st century. They cannot be justified. They deserve condemnation. The preservation of the Non-Proliferation Treaty demands an unequivocal commitment to their abolition . . . This is a moral challenge, a legal challenge and a political challenge. That multiple-based challenge must be met by the application of our humanity.

In his address the following year, Archbishop Martino said:

> The most perilous of all the old Cold War assumptions carried into the new age is the belief that the strategy of nuclear deterrence is essential to a nation's security. Maintaining nuclear deterrence into the 21st century will not aid but impede peace. Nuclear deterrence prevents genuine nuclear disarmament. It maintains an unacceptable hegemony over non-nuclear development for the poorest half of the world's population. It is a fundamental obstacle to achieving a new age of global security.

The Holy See spokesman again called for 'the abolition of nuclear weapons through a universal, non-discriminatory ban with inspection by a universal authority'.

At the 2005 Non-Proliferation Treaty (NPT) Review Conference, the Holy See made it clear that nuclear deterrence, in the modern context, cannot claim any moral legitimacy. Archbishop Celestino Migliore, Permanent Representative of the Holy See at the UN, stated:

> When the Holy See expressed its limited acceptance of nuclear deterrence during the Cold War, it was with the clearly stated condition that deterrence was only a step on the way towards progressive nuclear disarmament. The Holy See has never countenanced nuclear deterrence as a permanent measure, nor does it today when it is evident that nuclear deterrence drives the development of ever newer nuclear arms, thus preventing genuine nuclear disarmament.

Archbishop Migliore warned that the new threat of global terrorism must not be allowed to undermine the precepts of international humanitarian law. In addition, 'nuclear weapons, even so-called "low-yield" weapons, endanger the processes of life and can lead to extended conflict'.

Nuclear weapons assault life on the planet, they assault the planet itself, and in so doing they assault the process of the continuing development of the planet. The preservation of the Non-Proliferation Treaty demands an unequivocal commitment to genuine nuclear disarmament.

I interpret all these statements to mean that the Holy See's position on nuclear weapons can now be stated as follows:

Because the nuclear weapons States have decisively shown that they consider nuclear weapons permanent instruments in their military doctrine, the Holy See has withdrawn the limited acceptance it gave to nuclear weapons during the Cold War. In the eyes of the Catholic Church, nuclear weapons are evil and immoral and must be eliminated as a precondition to obtaining peace.

I hope my remarks have answered the question posed to this panel: 'What morally responsible approaches should be taken to prevent nuclear proliferation?' My answer, in short, is: the only morally responsible approach is the elimination of all nuclear weapons. How is it possible, in the name of morality, for some states to aggrandize unto themselves the right to maintain nuclear weapons while proscribing their acquisition by others? I do not have time here to discuss the illogic and impracticality of such a proposition. Rather, I am concentrating on the morality of the question. A two-class world, of nuclear haves and have-nots, is, in addition to being unsustainable, grossly immoral. I hope the American Catholic bishops, who have demonstrated great leadership in the past, will soon state this unequivocally.

# 4 Can Deterrence Be Just in the Twenty-first Century?

## DAVID FISHER

Twenty years ago I wrote a book entitled *Morality and the Bomb* in which I sought to provide an ethical justification for nuclear deterrence.[1] At the time we were still in the midst of the Cold War and the Western democracies faced the threat posed by a hostile Marxist totalitarian regime in the Soviet Union. In those tense circumstances, nuclear deterrence appeared to offer a way of stabilizing relations between two ideologically opposed power blocs that might otherwise have resorted to force. Nuclear deterrence thus appeared to play an indispensable role in helping keep the peace in the Cold War era.

For some, the pacific effect of deterrence appeared sufficient ethical justification on its own for deterrence. Deterrence works. It prevents war. That alone suffices to justify it and it is best not to enquire too closely how this is achieved.

But that was too easy an answer. The pacific effect of deterrence might be a necessary part of its justification but is not sufficient because there is an unavoidable link between deterrence and use. That connection did not need to be explicit, still less did it require the regular utterance of sabre-rattling holocaustal threats. But mutual deterrence did only work because there was at least some uncertainty in the mind of each side that nuclear weapons might be used. That uncertainty over use induced the restraint on behaviour that ensured that there was no resort to military force.

A deterrent threat is credible because the possibility of use has not been entirely excluded. But if any use were morally impermissible, then use should be excluded, for that is, after all, what impermissible means. Because of this intimate connection between deterrence and use, deterrence could only therefore be ethically permissible if there were an ethically permissible use of nuclear weapons. If any use was impermissible, so would be deterrence.

Devastating direct attacks on cities instantly causing hundreds of thousands or even millions of deaths of innocent civilians appeared impossible to reconcile with the just-war principles of proportion and discrimination, the former requiring that the harm caused by military action should be proportionate to the good to be achieved; the latter seeking to minimize civilian casualties. To be ethically permissible, a targeting policy would, therefore, need to eschew counter-city strikes because of the enormous civilian casualties that would inevitably result. The policy should instead be based on a counter-combatant targeting policy. The targets should primarily be military forces and their supporting infrastructure, including military–industrial infrastructure.

Such a policy could be ethically permissible. It could also provide an effective and credible underpinning for deterrence since such military and related assets were those most valued by the dictators whom we were seeking to deter, and whose threatened destruction would be most likely to dissuade them from aggressive action. By contrast, such tyrants typically showed scant regard for the fate of their own populace, as the signal failure of area bombing to dissuade Hitler from his aggression had amply demonstrated.

On such grounds I concluded that a minimal deterrent posture, based on a counter-combatant targeting policy and with stockpiles vastly reduced from the excessive holdings of the early 1980s, could be ethically permissible. The question addressed in this chapter is whether such arguments still work in the vastly changed circumstance of today. Can deterrence be just in the twenty-first century?

Twenty years on we live in a very different world. The Cold War has long since gone. We no longer face a hostile Marxist Soviet state. If not yet an established Western-style democracy, Russia is, however haltingly, moving towards democracy. President Putin is an ally, a friendly face at G8 Summits, such as that held in 2005 in Edinburgh to address global poverty.

When the Berlin Wall came down in 1989, some of my continental colleagues in NATO where I then worked believed peace was about to break out everywhere, removing the need for military alliances and force postures. Sadly, such optimism proved unfounded. Indeed, in the 15 years since the end of the Cold War, British Forces have been engaged in far more military operations than in the preceding 15, with deployments as far afield as Afghanistan and Iraq.

But the nature of the threats we now face is very different. The most pressing threat currently faced is from terrorism. Concern remains over threats posed by potentially hostile regional powers, perhaps armed with weapons of mass destruction, and the potential for regional confrontations to escalate into large-scale conflicts. The number of nuclear weapons states is increasing, with the recent public addition to the nuclear fold of Pakistan and India. There is continuing concern over the nuclear weapon threshold states such as North Korea and, most worryingly at present, Iran. But we no longer face a strategic threat to national survival of the kind that Soviet Russia once presented. So in these changed circumstances, can deterrence still be ethically justified?

In assessing the ethics of deterrence, the framework provided by the just-war tradition still provides by far the most useful tool. This prescribes that war is only permissible if: undertaken with right authority, as a last resort, for the sake of a just cause and in an expectation that the overall balance of good achieved would outweigh the harm. These are the so-called *jus ad bellum* conditions. The just-war tradition further prescribes that in the conduct of the war, due regard must be paid to the principles of proportion and discrimination, requiring that any use of force must be proportionate to the objective to be achieved and minimize civilian casualties.[2] The particular challenges presented by these conditions for nuclear deterrence have traditionally revolved around the closely related questions of whether any cause could justify nuclear use and whether nuclear use could ever be proportionate and discriminate.

The first hurdle is thus whether there could be a just cause for deterrence. Protecting democracy from the aggressive ambitions of a Marxist dictatorship might constitute a just cause. But what of the threats we face now?

There is a very immediate threat from terrorism, particularly that posed by Islamic extremists. There is also a concern that such terrorists might have or acquire chemical, biological or even crude nuclear devices and threaten their use against Western cities. This is cause for serious concern. But could nuclear deterrence work against such threats? There are two main problems with this.

First, deterrence in the Cold War presupposed a substantial degree of rationality on the part of each side. Deterrence worked because each side was assumed to be rational and so would be deterred from reckless action by the threat of the dire damage that would be inflicted against them. This was not just theory but worked in practice, as demonstrated during the Cuban missile crisis. Russia blustered but backed off. Even the US made secret concessions over nuclear bases in Turkey, as subsequently became public knowledge. Despite all the pressures, both sides refrained from action that might lead to nuclear use.

It is not, however, clear that a suicide bomber armed with a nuclear device would be amenable to such rational calculations. Indeed, as Michael Clarke has suggested: 'Terrorist groups would hardly be deterred by nuclear threats; indeed the mentality of the suicide bomber would probably rejoice at the prospect of provoking an incoming nuclear strike against many innocent others.'[3]

A second difficulty is that a nuclear-armed terrorist may have encroached upon our own territory, perhaps be hiding in a major city. Terrorists do not usually own territory, the role of the Taliban in Afghanistan being somewhat unusual in this respect. There may, therefore, be no territorial target that can be threatened. But a nuclear threat against the terrorists them-selves could thus pose a direct threat to our own citizens or those of our allies and so its utterance would be self-deterring. The threat would be likely to lack credibility.

Let us consider next the risk presented by regional powers armed with weapons of mass destruction. Concern over such powers has, for example, been cited by the French government as one of the reasons they have decided to retain and modernize their nuclear weapons.[4]

The term 'weapons of mass destruction' may make it sound as if a nuclear counter-threat could readily be justified since it suggests that all the weapons have an equally devastating effect to those of nuclear weapons. But it is more enlightening to unpack the term into nuclear, biological and chemical weapons since the weapons have very different characteristics.

Use of chemical and biological weapons, particularly in pop-ulation centres, could be horrific. The weapons may, moreover, in the longer term be further developed and perhaps allied with more sophisticated delivery systems than are currently avail-able. Nonetheless, the amount of damage caused by any nuclear use is generally accepted to be of a different order of magnitude from that caused by biological or chemical weapons, however unpleasant the latter may be. So the first question to address is whether a nuclear threat could be justified to deter use of chemical or biological weapons.

If, as during the Cold War, nuclear deterrence has been justi-fied on other grounds, such as the threat of Soviet aggression, it may be legitimate to exploit the uncertainty that nuclear possession inevitably engenders. A nuclear power can thus perhaps legitimately argue that a state contemplating use of chemical or biological weapons would have to take into account the possibility of nuclear use in retaliation. And that may have a successful deterrent effect. Deterrence against chemical or biological threats may thus constitute a legitimate secondary justification. The key question is, however, whether a threat presented by chemical or biological weapons could constitute the prime justification for nuclear possession.

It is sometimes argued that nuclear weapons can only deter nuclear use. But that was never part of classical deterrence theory. NATO never espoused a 'no-first-use' policy, and nuclear deterrence was designed to deter not only nuclear attack but also major conventional aggression.

Another misconception is that nuclear weapons could not be justified against chemical or biological weapons because the amount of damage caused by nuclear use would be disproportionate to the damage caused by chemical or biological weapons. But in the just-war tradition proportion is not a relation between damage levels threatened. This mistake led some to suppose during the heyday of deterrence theory that for deterrence to work we had to threaten more damage to an adversary than he could threaten to us. This led the theorists to suppose it necessary to pile up ever-increasing levels of threatened damage, including direct threats to populations, to underpin deterrence. But such an escalation of threats, usually inevitably risking massive damage to ourselves, far from enhancing could undermine the credibility of deterrence. The theoretical underpinning was, moreover, simply mistaken. For deterrence, in fact, works if the damage threatened is sufficient to convince an aggressor to refrain or desist from aggression. We do not need to threaten more damage than he can, but just enough to dissuade him.

The dyadic relation of proportionality is rather between the damage caused by military action and the good to be achieved or evil to be averted thereby. So if our national survival were threatened by an aggressor prosecuting his aggression with conventional weapons supported by chemical or biological weapons, a nuclear threat might be justified.

The difficulty with this justification for nuclear possession to counter biological or chemical threats is that the most likely threat of biological or chemical use is at present posed by a rogue regional power. Our primary objective is to prevent such states from acquiring these weapons through effective arms control and counter-proliferation strategies. But if these do not work, what kind of threats might such a power present through use of biological or chemical weapons?

A rogue regional state is unlikely to be in a position in the foreseeable future to pose a direct territorial threat to the United Kingdom through conventional aggression backed up by use of chemical or biological weapons, although the development of a capability to pose a direct threat with such weapons cannot be excluded in the longer term. The more likely foreseeable threats would, therefore, be to our deployed Forces operating overseas or against our cities through the local operation of agents of the rogue state. The question is whether nuclear use would represent a proportionate and credible response to such threats. On balance, other options, such as robust and prompt conventional action, might be deemed more appropriate and more likely to succeed in preventing or countering such chemical or biological use. For it is very difficult to envisage in such scenarios how the massive harm caused by nuclear use would be outweighed by the good to be achieved thereby.

The crux of the dilemma is that any use of nuclear weapons, however restrained and discriminate, would have devastating effects. Nuclear weapons are in a class of their own. That is, of course, why nuclear deterrence is effective. It has transformed the nature and cost of war. But such dire threats can only be ethically justified to counter extreme risks. So the only kind of just cause that might justify nuclear deterrence is a grave threat to national survival or vital national interests. This was, of course, always the underlying assumption during the Cold War period. It is perhaps conceivable that in the longer term biological or chemical weapons could be developed that could pose such a threat. But such a strategic threat is most likely to be presented by a power itself equipped with nuclear weapons.

There are a growing number of nuclear weapon states, and growing concern that potentially unfriendly regional powers such as Iran, may acquire them and the ballistic missiles needed to deliver them at long range. But none of these states currently possesses such a capability nor presents anything like a strategic threat to our survival or vital national interests.

So does that mean that nuclear deterrence can no longer be justified? That is not necessarily so since we are framing a defence posture for the next 30 to 40 years – the likely lifespan of a deterrent replacement. In such a timescale there could be risks of large-scale regional conflicts, perhaps involving newly emerging regional superpowers, that could have global implications. It can hardly be excluded from the realm of the possible that a strategic threat might re-emerge over such a long period and from quarters that we cannot currently foresee.

Against this it is argued that the improvement in international relations since the end of the Cold War is not just a short-term but systemic change and that a threat to national survival will not, therefore, re-emerge within the lifetime of a replacement system.[5] But such confident projections of the present and recent past into the future have seldom proved reliable predictors of the future. It was just such simplistic inductive reasoning that led to the presumption of peace prevailing for 30 years after the First World War, so leading to our lack of preparation to counter Hitler's aggression. Such reasoning conversely led virtually all commentators to presume that the Soviet threat would continue for far longer than it did and so fail to predict the fall of the Berlin Wall; and equally fail to predict the rise of militant Islamic terrorism.

So nuclear deterrence could still be justified as an insurance against a re-emergence of a threat to national survival or vital national interests, however unlikely that might seem at present. Nor would such insurance against a low probability but devastating risk necessarily be irrational, as the inhabitants of Lousiana suffering the effects of the failure to invest over many years in their sea defences might now testify. Moreover, nuclear possession justified on such grounds could, as noted earlier, still have a secondary beneficial effect by inducing uncertainty and hence caution in the mind of a rogue state contemplating biological or chemical use.

But even if there might still be a potential just cause for deterrence, all the other conditions of the just-war theory would also need to apply for deterrence to be ethically permissible. That would mean, in particular, that our strategy for use would need to comply with the principle of proportion – requiring that the good to be achieved should outweigh the harm caused by military action – and the principle of discrimination.

The principle of discrimination is sometimes interpreted, as Brian Wicker argues in his chapter, as imposing an absolute prohibition on military action that would involve any direct threat to the lives of non-combatants. If such an absolutist ethical stance is combined with a strategic assumption that the efficacy of deterrence is necessarily underpinned by a holocaustal threat of 'final retaliation',[6] it might appear that a powerful argument can be presented against nuclear deterrence. The proponent of deterrence is faced, in effect, with a Catch 22 dilemma: what he is proposing is either immoral or it will not work.

Can we escape from this dilemma? I believe we can. For it is based on a curious amalgam of what one might call 'right-wing strategy' from the depths of the Cold War and 'left-wing morality'. Neither the ethics nor the strategy seems to me to be right.

To treat the principle of discrimination as an absolute prohibition – admitting no exception – on military action directly inflicting civilian casualties is in the view of many just-war commentators to set an impossibly high standard. It would also prohibit not only nuclear deterrence but most forms of conventional warfare. The absolutist over-simplifies the complexities of our moral life where principles may conflict and it may not always be possible to hold fast to a principle without exception. We may – through no fault of our own – be faced with choices between actions each involving harm; and where the only 'right' thing to do is to choose the course of action that involves least harm. Such agonizing moral choices may be particularly difficult to avoid in war. Within the just-war tradition as it has been developed for most of its history, the principle of discrimination is, accordingly, not afforded absolute status but is rather viewed as an important additional constraint to that of proportion, requiring that action should be taken to minimize non-combatant casualties.

Even so interpreted, the constraints of proportion and discrimination remain very demanding. They would, in particular, require us publicly to eschew counter-city targeting since it is impossible to reconcile such counter-population attacks with the just-war requirements that military action should be proportionate and minimize civilian casualties. Our strategy would need instead to be based on an explicit counter-combatant targeting policy, holding at risk military and related assets.

The argument that any such attempt to constrain nuclear use for ethical reasons would undermine the effectiveness of deterrence is based on strategic assumptions which, as noted earlier, are mistaken. Far from undermining the effectiveness of deterrence, a counter-combatant targeting policy would enhance the credibility of deterrence. For the effectiveness of deterrence does not depend on a willingness to engage in ever-escalating counter-population strikes. Indeed, the dictators whom we are most likely to wish to deter in the post-Cold War period typically show scant regard for their populations. They are much more likely to be impressed by a threat to the military and related assets, including military–industrial assets, on which they depend for their power and whose threatened destruction is thus most likely to deter them. A counter-combatant targeting policy is thus not only required for deterrence to be ethically permissible. It is also essential to retain the credibility of deterrence in the post-Cold War era.

This latter consideration has not been lost on the French government. In June 2001 President Chirac announced a change in targeting policy:

> Deterrence must also enable us to deal with the threats to our vital interests that regional powers armed with weapons of mass destruction could pose . . . In this case the choice would not be between the total annihilation of a country and doing nothing. The damage to which a possible aggressor would be exposed would be directed above all against his political, economic and military power centres.[7]

In explaining this shift, Chirac's adviser, Henri Bentégeat noted that:

> Deterrence has been adapted to remain credible within the enduring framework of a policy of non-use . . .[8]

> We don't intend to develop battlefield weapons as the *force de frappe* is a political deterrent; instead we rely on a diversified payload that can spare an adversary's population and cities.[9]

These shifts in policy are to be welcomed, although it is left unclear from these gnomic pronouncements whether counter-city strikes have been excluded altogether. Clarity on this is required if a deterrent posture is to be ethically permissible.

## Conclusion

Deterrence based on a declared counter-combatant targeting policy could thus be ethically permissible as an insurance against the re-emergence of a threat to our national survival or vital interests. Utterance of threats or current targeting activity and planning are neither required nor appropriate to underpin such a long-term insurance policy. Moreover, the number of weapons held and their explosive power would need to be consistent with the avowed counter-combatant targeting policy and so substantially below current stockpiles in order to represent a genuinely minimum deterrent. The deterrence posture should be existential, solely designed to furnish a sombre calculation at the back of the mind of any power that might otherwise be tempted to use force in an age that the nuclear knowledge alone has rendered irrevocably nuclear.

Such a deterrent posture for the twenty-first century could be ethically permissible. Whether the premium is worth paying for such an insurance policy will clearly depend on both the absolute cost and the opportunity cost within the defence programme of a replacement system. These issues are addressed elsewhere in the book. My own view is that if a reasonable price were available, the insurance premium would be worth paying in an uncertain and still dangerous world. But at this point considerations of ethics yield to those of affordability and prudence.

*Note: The views expressed in this paper are those of the author and do not represent official Government policy or thinking.*

# 5 Is There a Case for a British Deterrent in the Twenty-first Century?

## BRIAN WICKER

### I

If Britain is to retain nuclear weapons this will presumably be for deterrence, not for fighting nuclear wars. So any case for retention must revisit the nuclear deterrence debate in the light of the changed circumstances of the twenty-first century. Who is to be deterred, and how?

Before we answer this question, however, a deeper one has to be asked: does nuclear deterrence *entail* that the deterrer has to be willing, as a last resort, intentionally to kill the innocent, that is to murder them? After all, as Lee Butler has said, nuclear deterrence 'holds guilty the innocent as well as the culpable'.[1] Hence, if the answer is 'Yes', then nuclear deterrence must be abandoned, since murdering the innocent is simply forbidden to human beings, because it is impossible for it to be compatible with justice; and so too must be any *willingness* to murder them.[2] Given that nuclear deterrence requires the deterrer to be willing, without bluffing, to inflict 'unacceptable damage' on the opponent, in order to scare him from attacking; and given that in the past such a requirement has been defined, rightly or wrongly, as destroying many of the opponent's inevitably innocent population;[3] and given also that a British government once thought it necessary to equip itself with means to make possible a nuclear attack on Moscow (the Chevaline system); it is clearly incumbent on any advocate of a British deterrent for the present century to show unambiguously that he is not willingly committed to *any* future murderous act.

I go into this question only to note one or two key points. First, the term 'willingness' is needed in order to meet the objection that the deterrer does not *intend* to commit murder, since here and now he does not need to harbour any intentions at all as to what he will do in the future: he is merely leaving the opponent in uncertainty about his intentions while equipping himself with the means to do whatever may be 'necessary' later. Yet even if the deterrer does not here and now harbour any intention, even conditionally, to respond with murder to an attack which has not yet come, he does have to be willing to do whatever he calculates he needs to do to ensure that his deterrent deters. Hence the deterrer has to be *willing* to inflict whatever level of 'unacceptable damage' he calculates is needed for this purpose.

Second, it can be no excuse that the deterrer's true intention is to 'keep the peace', or to 'prevent war'. For even if this were the purpose of his deterrent, and his deterrent did indeed help to prevent war, such a 'purpose' or objective is not something he can be said to *intend*, since preventing war is not an action which he can intend to do.[4] On the contrary, what matters is the *action(s)* the deterrer proposes to undertake in pursuit of this laudable purpose. Clarity about the intention with which the deterrer proposes to *act* is crucial to any assessment of his strategy.[5]

Third, the deterrer's choice of exclusively 'counter-force' targets, avoiding centres of innocent populations, cannot get him off the hook. For targeting is no sure indication of the intentions implicit in a deterrence policy. The key point is that *whatever action you want to make the adversary fear is what you intend to do*.[6] Thus, if as a last resort you want to make the adversary fear (say) the destruction of his cities, or a segment of his non-combatant population, then destroying these is what you have to be willing to do – however carefully you presently point your weapons for the time being only against 'counter-force' targets. And the same goes for any other definition of what you calculate will count for him as 'unacceptable damage'. The question of what sort and scale of damage is calculated to be 'unacceptable' is therefore crucial. Yet being willing to inflict it must *exclude* intentionally killing innocents. Simply deciding in advance not to hit civilian population centres is not nearly enough to satisfy this requirement. For one thing, subsequent indiscriminate radiation effects on the innocent and the unborn have also to be excluded. For another, there is always the temptation to override, in the heat of conflict, any well-intentioned limits with which it was begun, and falling for this temptation must equally be excluded. But how? Could (say) the 'carpet bombing' of cities during the course of the Second World War have been reliably excluded in advance? Certainly the Allies did not intend to do it at the beginning; but in the end they found themselves persuaded there was no alternative.[7] And finally, aiming at 'counter-force' targets only, within centres of civilian population, does not necessarily mean that the collateral civilian casualties are not intended.[8] To put the matter bluntly, whatever its targeting policy, no government that arrogates to itself the right to possess nuclear weapons can be trusted to keep a promise never to use them against the innocent.

Some indication of the British government's current calculations, concerning the scale of 'unacceptable damage' it feels necessary to be willing to inflict, appeared recently in an article by Michael Portillo in the *Sunday Times*.[9] While Secretary of State for Defence he visited one of Britain's Trident submarines, to see at first hand how it worked. He presumably knew at the time what the government envisaged by way of the 'unacceptable damage' we had to be willing to do. And being no longer in charge of this strategy, he perhaps felt free to say what it really was, instead of wrapping it up in 'government-speak' designed to avoid saying clearly what the necessary *actions* would consist of. And this is what he wrote:

> You may not have given much thought to the proper manner of initiating Armageddon. I gave the button a little stab as one might when pressing nine for an outside line. Be warned, reader, you need to press hard and long. My effete attempt to obliterate our foes led the system to enter an abort sequence . . .

If Portillo's article is to be taken seriously, then the 'unacceptable damage' Britain has to be willing to undertake seems to consist in 'initiating Armageddon' by 'obliterating our foes'. Even this language is not as precise as one would like about Britain's proposed actions. But the general outlines are clear: the emphasis seems to be on indiscriminate 'obliteration'.[10] And given that, on the only occasions thus far when nuclear weapons have been used in wartime, obliteration of thousands of innocents occurred, it is surely reasonable to conclude that, as the ultimate last resort when all else has failed, this is what we would still be willing to do, in order to make 'our foes' sufficiently afraid not to attack us.[11] This impression is reinforced further by the consideration that at an earlier stage in the development of nuclear deterrence there was no doubt that cities were to be attacked, since the inaccuracy of the delivery systems and the huge size of the warheads made such a policy unavoidable. Has anybody from within the policy-making elite ever uttered a word of remorse, let alone contrition, for Britain's having once gone along with this clearly murderous strategy?

## II

Nuclear deterrence is commonly discussed by appealing to 'just-war' ethical criteria. But this appeal is not as straightforward as it may seem. For like any other branch of ethics, 'just-war' thinking is affected by prevalent ethical assumptions. For example, much modern 'just-war' thinking is couched in consequentialist terms, according to which the goodness or badness of a course of action is to be judged by its results.[12] In this chapter I want to distinguish *consequentialist* just-war theory from what I shall call *classical* just-war theory. The two are poles apart.

It is tempting to think of just-war ethics in consequentialist terms because of its kinship with military strategy. For strategy, almost by definition, confines itself to the discussion of consequences. How best should I protect my country from potential enemies? Well, a good strategy is one which results in my country being successfully defended. So a strategy as such does not have to confront questions like: are the actions which its adoption requires, for the defence of my country, *just* actions? For as long as the strategy successfully protects my country from attack, the actions involved in it will, strategically speaking, be things it is 'good', i.e. advantageous, to do. But of course just-war theory is not about strategy: it is a branch of ethics. That is to say, it is about doing *just* things, not simply advantageous ones.

The problem is that there are people who think of ethics too as a strategy: i.e., it is simply about assessing the most beneficial consequences of our actions. A good action will then be one that has the best outcome: that is, offers the biggest balance of good over bad consequences. The 'just-war' criteria *can* be discussed in these terms. A *just-war* will then be one in which observance of these criteria yields the maximum practicable benefits, not just for my country but for other people's too. Of course, in the course of waging it some innocent civilians may have to be murdered. But if the overall outcome is favourable, and the disadvantageous things done are not preposterously disproportionate, then the war will turn out to have been *justified* despite the murders. The same goes for a deterrence policy: it too will be a policy that is *justified* or not according to its advantageous outcome: e.g., the absence of war. And nobody should be in any doubt that war is an evil of such colossal proportions that almost everything good is worth doing to prevent it.

My point is that such a 'justification' marks a decisive breach with the classical just-war tradition, which was always about the justice or otherwise of our actions, a few of which are simply incompatible with the common human good, or the 'natural law'.[13] Intentionally killing the innocent, or murder, is one of these intrinsically unjust acts. So, if a strategy entails, among other things, the action of intentionally killing the innocent, then, on classical grounds, it must be an unjust strategy. I call this the *classical* theory of just-war because it derives largely from the virtue ethics associated with Aristotle and Aquinas, rather than the consequentialist ethic which has emerged in the modern period. Today many people dispute the classical interpretation of the just-war criteria. For example, they 'justify' some intentional killing of the innocent as a means to a good end, quoting examples to prove the point. *Minimizing*, rather than excluding, the intentional killing of the innocent then becomes the consequentialist interpretation of the just-war criterion of 'discrimination'.[14] To do this it is furthermore necessary drastically to modify the principle of 'double effect', according to which it is licit to do something that is otherwise forbidden only if the forbidden thing is an *unintended* (albeit unavoidable) side effect of the action. For the 'double effect' principle of side effects is incompatible with consequentialism, since the latter rests on a notion that 'it does not make any difference to a man's responsibility for an effect of his action which he can foresee, that he does not intend it'.[15] Whereas consistent application of the double effect concept of side effects, and of the concept of *intention* which underlies it, is an absolutely necessity for classical just-war thinking.

This point is illustrated by the 'flattening' of the city of Cleves in the Second World War (see note 7). The city was crowded with refugees, as well as containing a significant number of German troops. In discussing this incident, Duncan Forrester suggests that flattening the city by blanket bombing 'was a *necessary* act, just according to the criteria of *ius in bello*'. But this conclusion is possible only if the act of bombing could be genuinely distinguished from its *consequences*; and describing the operation as 'blanket bombing' makes this impossible, since by this very definition the act included the killing, i.e. murder, of the innocent refugees. Only if those deaths were truly describable as the unintended, albeit unavoidable, *consequences* of the act, and not part of the act itself, could the 'double effect' justification apply. And the implication of a consequentialist just-war theory is that this distinction is impracticable. Hence, according to this theory of just-war ethics, only the consequences count: for the act and its consequences are all one, and the classical concept of the 'double effect' is undermined. It is a plausible theory because there may be no one true description of what is being done. Yet there is always the temptation, necessarily to be resisted, to misdescribe what has been done in order to avoid blame. This is a philosophical issue of the greatest importance, which it is unfortunately impossible to go into it in detail here.

Finally, use of notions such as '*prima facie*' duties which, even if they involve us in evil actions, may in certain circumstances become duties *sans phrase*, is also incompatible with classical just-war thinking, for it is only another way of saying that we may do evil that good may come.[16] And of course justifying deterrence by way of the (alleged but inevitably unproven) consequence that war is prevented, can be yet another way of using the just-war principles in a quite *unclassical* fashion, by misuse of the concept of *intention* – as I have already suggested.

## III

So much for the ethics of 'just deterrence'. The question now is whether there could be a new kind of deterrence which fully respected the classical just-war tradition while confronting the challenges of the twenty-first century. I think this problem can be divided into two parts: first of all dealing with possible threats from regional 'rogue states', such as Iran or North Korea; and second, dealing with terrorism by non-state actors such as al-Qaeda. The two kinds of case are significantly different from each other.

Nuclear deterrence was developed as a means of coping with the Cold *War*. That is to say, the context was a true Clausewitzian duel between two sides,[17] each of which could be properly construed as a collective personality capable of making rational decisions, such as deciding that it would be futile to attack the other side for fear of retaliation by way of 'unacceptable damage'. Classical just-war theory, with its criterion of 'lawful authority' for going to war, takes this concept of sovereignty, and its capacity for making decisions, for granted. What is more, the very idea of national 'self-defence' (UN Charter Article 51), which was the bedrock of nuclear deterrence policy, rests on the perception that what is at stake is the security of a collective personality, such as a UN member state, in which a sovereign authority (in modern conditions the national government) can act for the whole. This must also be the basis, then, of deterring a 'rogue state'. That state, the strategy assumes, is capable of rational decision about how to conduct itself in the duel of prospective war.

Now nuclear deterrence of a 'rogue state' which already possesses, or has aspirations to acquire, weapons of mass destruction, especially nuclear weapons, is no more than an extension of the familiar Cold War theory of deterrence, whereby a state is deterred by the rational fear of what will happen to it if it chooses to attack. Nevertheless, the rogue state scenario has a feature foreign to the later stages of the 'Cold War' between two roughly equal superpowers: namely that it may not have more than a few nuclear weapons with which to attack, or retaliate against, a much superior foe. (In its early stages, Cold War deterrence of course was also like this. And at least until the end of the Cold War French nuclear strategy was still predicated on this principle: *du faible au fort*.) The question then is: can the deterrer of today effectively confine his deterrent to legitimate 'counter-force', or 'counter-combatant' targets, in a way that was impossible in the early Cold War scenario? And can he be counted on not to attack the innocent if things go 'hot' and the deterrer has actually to carry out his threats? In the crisis of deterrence failure, is the promise of confining destruction to counterforce targets worth the paper it is written on?

As I have already said, such a deterrent must go much further than merely adopting in advance a declaratory policy of not *targeting* centres of the rogue state's civilian population, for as we have seen, targeting is not an adequate index of a deterrer's intentions. The deterrent must be effective without the deterrer *wanting or intending* consequences which harm the rogue state's innocent civilian population, and (as we have seen already) these *consequences* must be distinguishable from the *action*s proposed to be done by the deterrer. And of course, if the rogue state has placed his counter-force targets amidst civilian-populated areas, just deterrence cannot be created simply by aiming nuclear weapons only at combatant targets within those civilian areas, unless the civilian casualties within them would be genuinely *accidental consequences*, completely unnecessary to the deterrer's purpose in acting. As delivery systems become ever more accurate, such aiming at specific targets will indeed become more feasible (leaving aside the lethally indiscriminate radiation effects, which cannot be thus limited solely to counter-force targets) but, correspondingly, any failure to live up to the aspiration of preventing civilian casualties in practice becomes more blameworthy. So the question now is: would such a form of 'pure counter-force' deterrence actually deter a really determined rogue nuclear state?

There were powerful arguments for saying that, under Cold War conditions, this would be impossible: 'city-swapping' would have to be envisaged as part of any 'pure counter-force' deterrence.[18] That is to say, the deterrer would have to be willing to attack the enemy's cities in retaliation if, despite his scrupulosity in aiming his nuclear weapons only at only 'counter-force' targets, his own cities were being threatened with destruction by an enemy's pre-emptive nuclear attack. Is there any reason to suppose that this is not so in the case of a regional nuclear 'rogue state'?

Consider the Iran case. It is plausibly assumed by many who are in the know that Iran is not only aiming to develop nuclear weapons, but is also in the course of acquiring long-range missiles capable of hitting cities in Western Europe.[19] If this is so, there is a possibility that Iran might at some future time wish to initiate a nuclear attack on Europe, perhaps including London, with one or two of its nuclear-tipped missiles, as a means of helping some illicit cause it is pursuing. How could Britain deter Iran from doing this? Well, let us assume that diplomacy, economic sanctions, political pressure have failed, so that now deterrence itself is put to the test. If intelligence shows that Iran is now poised to attack, then a pre-emptive strike with very accurate missiles solely against Iran's nuclear assets might be regarded as legitimate self-defence. And this would be in accordance with a declaratory policy of attacking only 'counter-force' targets. But if Iran got wind of this imminent strike, it could in theory launch one of its missiles before the strike landed. How could it be deterred from even considering such an act? Surely only by Britain's being able and willing to inflict indubitably unacceptable damage, such that, however strong Iran's reason for attacking, it would in the end desist. It is at this point that an attack by Britain against an Iranian city (say, Tehran) might be calculated to be necessary, to make deterrence fully effective. However sincerely Britain had adopted in advance a policy of eschewing any such action, attacking a city might become irresistible at the crucial point.[20] This is why an in-advance declaratory policy of eschewing murder is not enough. For, given the prospect of some level of 'obliteration' (e.g. the destruction of London), such a policy cannot be expected to stick.

A bigger problem still comes when a 'rogue state' disintegrates into a 'failed state', which cannot be easily deterred because it has ceased to have an authority at its head with rational fears for itself. It is far from clear whether a failed state can be deterred. Consider a North Korea which had finally failed to feed its own people, and there ensued a serious rebellion in which the government lost control. We would then be confronted by a failed state with nuclear weapons. God knows how the world could, or should, deal with such an eventuality. Chaos would come again. The obvious point to make is that it is imperative that no nuclear-weapons state becomes a failed state. But is it possible to guarantee this? In any case, deterrence would have collapsed if the 'failed state' ceased to be rationally capable of being deterred from using its nuclear weapons by fear of the 'unacceptable damage' it would suffer.

If there is a valid case at all for nuclear deterrence, it will be put to the extreme test by the appearance of a failed state with nuclear weapons on its territory. There is no good reason to think that it would work. This is a powerful reason for trying to eliminate nuclear weapons altogether, in accordance with the obligations enshrined in Article 6 of the Nuclear Non-Proliferation Treaty.

The case is otherwise with the idea of using nuclear weapons to deter criminal gangs like al-Qaeda.[21] For here we do not have a clearly definable 'opponent' at all. The struggle is not a Clausewitzian duel between two rational sides. Here, whatever George W. Bush and his ilk may say, we cannot properly speak of a war. For war is defined by its being a duel between two sides, in which one side hopes to win and the loser has to accept that it has lost. A terrorist network, of which it is impossible clearly to distinguish the members, cannot constitute a distinct side in a duel, for it has no sovereign 'authority' which can take decisions in its name – not even, perhaps least of all, the decision that it has lost. Against it there can be no just war; only police action against criminality on a gigantic scale. In such a situation, nuclear deterrence cannot get a foothold, for it depends on the opponent's rational fear of being overwhelmed, and some members (God knows which ones) of the terrorist gang may not wish to avoid being overwhelmed, provided they can destroy the rest of the world as they go down in flames. If global criminality implies, as its corollary, a global system for fighting crime – in short, some kind of global police force – so be it. This would be just another element in the increasingly globalized nature of the twenty-first-century world, alongside global climate change, global corporations, global tourism, global communications and the Internet. Difficult though it is to imagine what this global crime-fighting system would look like, it is going to be necessary to create it. This is one of the consequences of taking an 'absolutist' ethical stance against nuclear deterrence. For the point of absolute prohibitions, for example on the intentional killing of the innocent, is that they *necessitate* radical changes in world order, whereas falling for the temptation of a more accommodating ethic relieves us of that urgent necessity. Talk of a 'war' on terrorism takes us back into familiar old-fashioned territory (we tend to imagine we know how to wage wars) whereas the reality is that we need to think ourselves beyond 'warfare' into the new and relatively uncharted waters of 'globalization'.[22]

If there is a case for Britain retaining its nuclear deterrent, it cannot be for dealing with terrorists, only (at best) with 'rogue states'. But as I have argued, even this prospect cannot eliminate the essentially murderous character of nuclear deterrence. Whether there is a real prospect of imminent danger to the survival of Britain or its 'vital interests' from such states is a matter of dispute. But even if there is, the ethical considerations I have outlined above have still to be faced. In my judgement, when they are so confronted, the essentially murderous – and thus forbidden – nature of nuclear deterrence in the twenty-first century becomes quite clear.[23]

# 6  If Our Enemies Have Nuclear Weapons, So Must We

## OLIVER KAMM

The debate over a possible replacement for the current Trident programme is distinctive for what it lacks more than for what it possesses. In the early 1980s, when the Church of England Synod considered the *Church and the Bomb* report, and the National Conference of Catholic Bishops in the United States issued its Pastoral Letter *The Challenge of Peace*, arguments over defence policy were dominated by the ethics of nuclear deterrence. The most prominent critics of an independent nuclear deterrent now ground their case in strategy rather than morality. The arguments of the anti-nuclear movement have long reflected an uneasy mix of the exhortatory, the apocalyptic and the pragmatic. Even the veteran campaigner and CND vice-president Bruce Kent, having argued vigorously but without success against nuclear weapons in the 1980s, now appears to stress the last of those considerations. In an interview assessing CND's historic influence, Kent argued: 'The philosophy of nuclear deterrence is inherently unstable and dangerous and CND can and should go on stating that nuclear weapons are no road to international peace and security.'[1]

If the strategy and philosophy rather than the morals of nuclear deterrence are at the forefront of debate, then so much the better. It is a good thing not because ethical argument about nuclear weapons is illegitimate, but because it is inconclusive. If you believe nuclear deterrence is an evil – even a contingently tolerable one – then you should work to eradicate it. Yet rereading the Church statements of a generation ago reveals a widespread acceptance of this premise allied to a curious diffidence in expounding it. For example, the Methodist Conference of 1983 considered a report, *Nuclear Disarmament – Some Theological Considerations*, that argued: 'We reflect on the mixture of unilateralist and multilateralist courses which the Bible, the life and death of Christ and the Christian tradition urge upon us.' I can understand that many Christians would regard as morally unconscionable a conditional threat to launch nuclear destruction. But the notion that Christian doctrine and tradition stipulate almost precisely the policies of the Labour Party under Michael Foot is a little harder to credit.[2] There are good reasons that attempts to apply the ethics of the Kingdom in the secular realm frequently end up more bathetic than prophetic. As Reinhold Niebuhr observed in 1952:

> Politics always aims at some kind of a harmony or balance of interest, and such a harmony cannot be regarded as directly related to the final harmony of love of the Kingdom of God. All men are naturally inclined to obscure the morally ambiguous element in their political cause by investing it with religious sanctity. This is why religion is more frequently a source of confusion than of light in the political realm. The tendency to equate our political with our Christian convictions causes politics to generate idolatry.[3]

In the political realm, every British government since 1945 has worked on the implicit assumption that if our enemies have nuclear weapons then so must we, as a deterrent. I hold that view too. I do not believe that threatening to do what is wrong is necessarily itself wrong. I do not believe that threatening nuclear destruction is wrong at all, if it serves the beneficial purpose of deterring aggression and safeguarding liberty. Nuclear deterrence is not only morally permissible, but as the Synod declared with its 1983 vote, 'it is the duty of HM Government and her allies to maintain adequate forces to guard against nuclear blackmail and to deter potential nuclear and non-nuclear aggressors'. No British government will retreat from that view. The only time a major party embraced nuclear pacifism in a General Election the outcome was electoral oblivion.

If opposition to a new independent deterrent focuses more closely on strategic rather than moral judgements, it makes for a more constructive and a necessary debate. Advocates and opponents of nuclear defence have often talked past each other rather than sought common premises. It is welcome that the new arguments for renouncing (or not replacing) British nuclear weapons are about means more than ends. Many who took no part in anti-nuclear campaigns of 20 or more years ago have concluded that there is no good case for a new generation of British nuclear weapons in a post-Cold War world. The Bishop of Oxford, Richard Harries, is one of those critics, and contributes his argument to this volume. In the political arena, perhaps the most notable convert is the former Conservative Defence Secretary, Michael Portillo.

These and other establishment figures do not argue that nuclear deterrence is futile, or immoral, or destructive of international comity. They concentrate on the British independent nuclear deterrent, and conclude that it is an extravagance whose *raison d'être* expired with the Soviet Union. It distorts our defence budget and our relationship with the United States. Replacing the current Trident programme will also undermine our credibility in countering nuclear proliferation.

This is a serious and seductive argument that suffers only from being the reverse of the truth. An independent deterrent has become more important since the Cold War, not less, as the relatively stable bilateral relationship between the superpowers has been superseded by new potential challengers. It does not follow that, because the most pressing defence issue of the new millennium has been an attack on the American mainland by 19 men armed only with box cutters and religious fanaticism, threats from hostile states have receded. The principal defence challenge of our age is the confluence of theocratic terrorism, weapons of mass destruction (an unhelpful portmanteau term, but one that is in common use), and states willing to be the intermediary between the two. We cannot anticipate what form these multiple threats will take over the next 20 years. It would be foolhardy to assume that the possibilities will be exhausted by the undeterrable terrorist with a 'dirty bomb' in a suitcase, or the residual risk of Russian nuclear weapons.

During the Cold War, the argument was that a second centre of nuclear decision-making within NATO strengthened deterrence. The Soviet leadership might in theory gamble that a US President would not sacrifice New York or Chicago for Paris or London, and would thus hold back from retaliating with strategic nuclear weapons to nuclear blackmail. NATO could mitigate the threat of blackmail by having another sovereign power – Britain in this case, as France stands outside NATO's integrated military command – with the ability to strike at Soviet cities with ballistic missiles.

This argument was not wrong, but it was minor, and the effect was marginal. Brutal and expansionist as they were, Soviet leaders were also sufficiently risk-averse not to wish to test the US commitment to Europe's defence, with or without a British nuclear force. The history of NATO doctrine in the Cold War was partly a succession of expedients to ensure that deterrence was 'credible': that military commanders would have the option of graduated responses to a nuclear threat, so that Soviet leaders would not be tempted to test the solidarity of NATO.

In our 'second nuclear age', the threats we face are different and less predictable. The US and its allies have a common interest with Russia in countering Islamist terrorism, and with China in containing North Korea. But beyond is an anarchic order in which regional powers and non-state actors complicate traditional notions of deterrence. Most potent of these threats are states for whom nuclear, chemical and biological weapons are, in President Bush's words, 'not weapons of last resort, but militarily useful weapons of choice'.

The failure to find weapons of mass destruction in Iraq has not diminished the force of the President's warning. Saddam Hussein did possess chemical weapons, and used them against Iranian troop concentrations in the Iran-Iraq war. By the end of the 1980s he possessed an implosion design for a nuclear weapon, and would surely have manufactured a nuclear capability if he could have stolen or bought enriched uranium from, say, North Korea. Even at the time of the Iraq War in 2003, Iraq did possess dual-use facilities that, according to Charles Duelfer of the Iraq Survey Group, could quickly have produced chemical and biological weapons. In the case of rogue states in future, we could not have the necessary degree of certainty of their disarmament, even with an intrusive system of inspections. As Professor Graham Pearson, of the Bradford University School of Peace Studies, has written, focusing on stockpiles of weapons is misconceived: 'In an aggressor state, there is no requirement to have such stockpiles as the national strategy is not one of having an ability to retaliate in kind but rather . . . to use chemical and biological weapons at a time of its choosing.'[4]

It is a common argument that the absence of weapons of mass destruction in post-Baathist Iraq undermined the case for war; I disagree with that view, but that is not the issue I am here taking up. What is more germane to this discussion is that Western powers had no real idea, at any time, of the military capabilities of an irrational despot. (If you doubt that Saddam was irrational, consider the fact that he launched three near-suicidal wars in 17 years, and that each almost destroyed his regime: Iran in 1974; Iran again in 1980; and the invasion and annexation of Kuwait in 1990.) This is the type of state that would be the most likely conduit by which Islamist terrorists might obtain even a rudimentary nuclear device, or biological or chemical agents. The greatest question of international politics is how we deal with these potential threats.

There is a respectable argument that the right course is diplomacy, agreement and law, on grounds of the utility of good global governance, and the limits – observed in Iraq – of military power. It is a much better argument than the old unilateralist notion that Britain might set a moral example to the world by renouncing its nuclear status. But it still bears scant relation to how the international order works. Seeking to sublimate regional conflict in international agreements is a noble venture and occasionally a useful one, but the ultimate guarantor of peace in a world lacking a sovereign international legal authority is the threat of superior force.

Representatives of the new pragmatic anti-nuclear stance in fact seem hesitant about pressing this argument too far, as they sometimes introduce a point of comparison between the sums spent on a replacement for Trident and public needs in the alleviation of poverty and hunger. But this appears to be rhetoric. The critics do not usually call for the money to be diverted to the overseas aid budget, but instead want it spent on conventional forces. This is where the argument becomes question-begging: it assumes in its premises ('We can defend ourselves adequately with conventional forces') its conclusion ('We do not need an independent nuclear deterrent'). But if an independent nuclear deterrent adds something qualitative to our defence for which there is no substitute, then the money must be better spent this way than on additional aircraft or tanks.

Does an independent deterrent in fact provide an extra dimension of security? It does, in circumstances we may not expect but ought prudently to anticipate. Consider a thought-experiment. When Argentina invaded the Falkland Islands in 1982, antinuclear campaigners were quick to point out that the independent nuclear deterrent had not deterred. This was true but superficial. Suppose that Argentina had been a nuclear-armed power too. Would the British government still have sent a task force to retake the islands? The likelihood would surely have been diminished, even with a low risk of direct nuclear exchange. Suppose further that Argentina had possessed nuclear weapons and – as the Labour Party then urged – Britain had not. In that case, it would have been inconceivable for any British government to seek to recapture the Falklands. Merely by possessing nuclear weapons and without any explicit threat of nuclear blackmail, a dictatorship would have won territories it coveted, by force of arms and in defiance of international law.

The initial instincts of the Reagan administration when the Falklands crisis broke were to mediate rather than take sides against the aggressor. Where the writ of collective security does not run, an aggressive state might rationally calculate (even if it were mistaken) that the US would stand aside. The domestic pressures for the US to do that are always present. As the analyst Colin Gray has noted: 'Americans may decide that while it is wise to remain Number One, they will remain Number One solely to protect Number One. It would not be sensible, but domestic politics are not ruled by strategic reason.'[5] Nuclear proliferation, or even just the suspicion of a rudimentary nuclear capability in the hands of a rogue state, exacerbates the problem.

The risk of nuclear blackmail by an emerging regional power is not negligible. It is as plausible as Saddam Hussein's annexation and plunder of Kuwait in 1990, which would have been irreversible had he possessed the ability to render Kuwait a radioactive wasteland. A nuclear deterrent allied to, but independent of, the US might in some circumstances cause an aggressor to reconsider, simply because it confers an additional and irreducible political counterweight not possessed by, say, Canada. That European capability cannot be left to France alone, for the reason it is doubtless impolitic to mention that gangster regimes in autocratic states have scant historical grounds for regarding France as an impediment to their ambitions.

Strengthening nuclear counter-proliferation measures is important, but the impact of a British nuclear renunciation would be minimal. The states most amenable to diplomatic pressure are not Iran or North Korea, but those such as South Africa (which voluntarily relinquished its nuclear capability) or Brazil that threaten no one. Israel has compelling independent reason not to commit to nuclear abolition; Pakistan will do so only if India does; India will not if China does not.

The debate on a British nuclear deterrent has suffered from the perception that it is bound up with the political fortunes of the current Labour government. Having been electorally crippled by its anti-nuclear policies in the 1980s, the Labour Party now wishes to avoid any hint of being soft on defence. But that is not an ignoble motivation. Parties of the Left, on both sides of the Atlantic, have a tradition of anti-totalitarianism and commitment to collective security. Labour governments took Britain into NATO and modernized the old Polaris fleet. Conversely, the last Conservative government was diffident about the exercise of military power, in that it acquiesced in Serb aggression against Bosnia's multi-ethnic democracy. Anti-nuclear campaigners would be wise to avoid assuming that the case against Trident's successor is a blow for progress against reaction, or even merely principle against expediency. There is a much stronger case for replacing the current generation of British nuclear weapons than there was for acquiring them in the first place.

# 7  Status Symbol or Weapon of War? What is Trident *For*?

## MICHAEL MCGWIRE

In 1957, the post-Suez Defence Review[1] ruled that nuclear weapons would provide the basis of British security. Our need for US assistance with the weapons delivery systems set in concrete a parallel foreign-policy decision. In future, London would take pains to be on the same side of the argument as Washington. Here we have the roots of the 'special relationship' with America, which over the years morphed into 'loyal vassal' and is today captured by the image of a powerless pillion passenger. Here, too, are the roots of Britain's present-day nuclear policy.

Trident is a single-purpose weapons platform, designed to deliver death and destruction to distant parts of the globe. That capacity is not trivial. Scaling up from Hiroshima and Nagasaki, a single Trident has the notional capacity to cause over 20 million instantaneous deaths. Which brings us to the question: is it in Britains's wider interests to retain its nuclear capability? There is danger in using Trident as shorthand for that capability, because it lures one into discussing the technicalities, timing and logistics of how the Trident system might be replaced, which the government is only too happy for us to do. Those are all secondary issues, however, which divert us from the pressing question of 'Does Britain need a nuclear capability?' – a question that was specifically ruled out from consideration by the 1998 Strategic Defence Review. It is pressing because we are presented with a fleeting window of opportunity, and windows of opportunity are critical to effecting political change. They are very rare and only arise when a conjunction of circumstances outweighs the inertia of established attitudes, assumptions and policies.

The emerging debate about Trident obsolescence is the primary circumstance in the present conjunction. Mounting dissatisfaction with Britain's role as pillion passenger to America is another. Public doubt about Blair's judgement, particularly where questions of foreign policy and defence are concerned, is a third. Meanwhile, the potential benefits of abandoning our nuclear capability are at a peak.

Windows of opportunity are spring-loaded to close. Think back to the second half of the 1990s and the unprecedented array of authoritative analyses and reports, mainly American, some international, all concluding that nuclear weapons imperiled humankind, all recommending their elimination. A common feature of those analyses was the range and calibre of the signatories, and the relevance of their political and professional expertise. The number of senior generals and admirals willing to go publicly on record was particularly notable. They included Air Force General Lee Butler, recently retired after four years in Command of US strategic nuclear forces, and Andrew Goodpaster, former Supreme Allied Commander, Europe. On this side of the Atlantic we had Field Marshal Michael Carver, former Chief of the Defence Staff. And of course, Robert McNamara, who had not only been US Secretary of Defence during the Cuban missile crisis, but 30 years later participated in the research conferences on the crisis, which revealed how close the superpowers had come to inadvertent nuclear war.

Why did this impressive body of professional opinion and analysis have no visible effect on the nuclear policy process in Washington – or, for that matter, in London? The answer was that the window of opportunity that opened wide following the overwhelming success of US conventional arms in the 1991 Gulf War had already closed by 1995, when those reports began to emerge. This was partly fate, such as the mortal illness of Les Aspin (US Secretary of Defence) and the notable absence of Presidential leadership. But it was mainly due to the weight of political and bureaucratic inertia, the strength of the Department's 'traditionalists', and the vested interests of the powerful nuclear weapons establishment – a conjunction that is not unknown in Britain. In short, do not expect US nuclear policy to change for the better. The key policy decisions were made during the first Clinton administration and will be followed through by the US nuclear weapons establishment. If Britain's nuclear policy originates in the wake of Suez, US policy originates in 1946, when negotiations on establishing a UN Atomic Energy Commission (the Baruch plan) were set up to fail, and duly did so.

Refocusing on Britain, in the 30-plus years following Suez, our all-consuming security concern was the Soviet Union's military capability, particularly the threat posed by its forces facing Western Europe. Having achieved, with immense effort, a nuclear capability, it was understandable that Britain would retain that capability, even though it was of no military significance and had no appreciable effect on NATO policy.

Today, we are 750 miles or more from the nearest areas of political turbulence. Anchored off the western coast of Europe, with allies or friends on all sides, Britain is unusually secure. Despite these enviable circumstances, the government tells us that our nuclear capability 'is likely to remain a necessary element of our security'. It declines to divulge the circumstances in which those weapons might be used, claiming it is advantageous to maintain uncertainty in the minds of possible opponents. This is, of course, nonsense. A central tenet of strategic theory is that the effectiveness of deterrence relies absolutely on the *certainty* of the response, which must be credible in both political and military terms.[2]

The uncertainty is in the government's mind; uncertainty about what the distant future holds. But is that sufficient reason to justify the retention of a nuclear capability? The question clamours for some kind of cost/benefit analysis. Instead, the government has chosen to rely on the concepts of sunk costs and hedging (which have a commonsense appeal), and on the politician's instinct that one shouldn't give up an asset without getting something in return – although no one can think of what that 'something' might be. Meanwhile, it is generally accepted that if we did not *already* possess nuclear weapons, Britain would *not* develop them, and there is a broad consensus that as we already have them – sunk costs – we might as well keep them – hedging. The trouble with this market-savvy, commonsense approach – a mix of 'come in handy' and 'better safe than sorry' – is that, while acknowledging the economic costs (about 5 per cent of the defence budget), there is no consideration of the political costs to Britain of its nuclear status.

There are the direct political costs of our close association with America, such as sharing world opprobrium when US policies are unpopular, but gaining little credit when they succeed. What is more serious (if less obvious), as a loyal vassal we find ourselves adopting, supporting, going along with, or remaining silent about US policies that are generated by US electoral politics, policies that reflect American domestic sectional interests, with little concern for wider national interests, and none at all for Britain's. But the largest political costs are indirect.

I will come back to these, but first let us deal with the 'political status' that is said to derive from a nuclear capability, and which is often claimed as a benefit. Unquestionably, status was an important policy consideration in the mid-1950s. By the end of the decade, Harold Macmillan was publicly justifying the money being spent on Britain's less-than-independent nuclear deterrent on the grounds that it gave Britain 'a place at the table' of Soviet–America nuclear arms negotiations. We had, however, lost that place by the end of the 1960s, when the superpowers turned to negotiations on strategic systems. Nuclear weapons became the lace curtains of Britain's political poverty.

By the 1980s, it was Germany that had Washington's ear in Europe, and Japan had it in the Far East. Britain, meanwhile, had difficulty in persuading Washington to help over the Falklands and was not even consulted when the US decided to invade Grenada. In 1990, London and Paris lost out to Bonn over German reunification, and again in 1993–94 over the decision to extend NATO. Britain and France were nuclear powers, Germany was not. In short, political status does not necessarily depend on a nuclear capability. It is a subjective concept and, to the extent that there is a link between political status and nuclear capability, it is situation-specific and depends on one's position on the international totem pole. As a general rule, the lower one's position, the greater the relative gain.

That being so, it is hard to see why Britain, a senior member of all the best international clubs, would lose political status (or its permanent seat on the Security Council) if it renounced its nuclear capability. While Washington would be irritated to lose a loyal vassal, in other quarters (including most of the Western world), if Britain were no longer seen as America's glove puppet, I am confident its political status would rise.

In sum, the present and future benefits of our nuclear weapons add up to their role as a hedge against uncertainty (a role that generates its own costs); and a questionable claim for enhanced political status.

Moving to the cost side of the equation, the government focuses attention on the economic costs of our nuclear capability (which are not prohibitive), but chooses to ignore political costs; both the *direct* political costs, such as our unhealthy dependence on the United States, and the more important *indirect* costs of opportunities forgone or excluded as a consequence of current policies – the things Britain could do and achieve if it did *not* have a nuclear capability: so-called 'opportunity costs', particularly in respect to the Non-Proliferation Treaty and to Britain's role in the world.

Let's start with the Non-Proliferation Treaty. At the time of the Treaty's inception in 1968 and for the next 25 years, the Non-Proliferation Treaty was immensely important and un-expectedly successful. The success was largely due to the nature of the Cold War world with its two camps, client states and the superpowers' common interest. In the US camp, skilful carrot-and-stick diplomacy persuaded most of the nuclear aspirants to fall into line, and the end of the Cold War brought a final surge of signatures, resulting in the Treaty being effectively universal.

Today, the Treaty is like a wisdom tooth that is rotten at its root, and the abscess is poisoning the international body politic. What went wrong? And what needs to be done to put it right? At the heart of the Treaty was a Grand Bargain. The *non-nuclear* signatories agreed to forgo the option of acquiring nuclear weapons, in exchange for unimpeded access to nuclear energy for non-military purposes, and a promise by the *nuclear-weapon* states on nuclear disarmament. As a consequence, the world at large would be able to enjoy the peaceful benefits of nuclear science, and the technologically advanced countries would have unrestricted commercial access to this lucrative market, with no danger of being forced into an arms race.

Embedded in the Treaty were two problems. One was 'dual use' – the fact that materials and technology required for legiti-mate peaceful purposes can also be used (diverted) to produce weapons. The other problem concerns the commitment to ultimate nuclear disarmament. To obtain the agreement of the non-nuclear members of the negotiating committee, the two superpowers had to accept this proviso, which was embodied in Article 6 of the Treaty. In 1968, with the strategic arms race already under way, the superpowers saw Article 6 as an empty aspiration and nothing to worry about. But 25 years later, the surprise ending of the Cold War gave Article 6 a whole new significance.

A notable deficiency in the Treaty's terms was partially remedied by the passage of time. Unlike the Chemical and Biological Conventions, the Non-Proliferation Treaty did not even mention, let alone prohibit, the *use* of nuclear weapons. US strategy was based on deterrence and predicated on a readiness to use nuclear weapons, and it refused to discuss any kind of prohibition. It still does. However, when the East–West confrontation ended without resort to such weapons, a tacit pledge was promoted to moral prohibition, a 'nuclear taboo' that has been respected (in deed, if not word) since the horrors of Hiroshima 60 years ago.

Come the end of the Cold War, the nuclear-weapon states sought the indefinite extension of the Non-Proliferation Treaty. This was agreed at the 1995 Treaty Review Conference, in return for a range of inducements to the non-nuclear states, which included the promise that the five-yearly Review Conferences would provide an engine for progress towards the goal of nuclear disarmament. But once the extension of the Treaty was in the bag, the failure of the NATO nuclear-weapon states to deliver on their promises was blatant.

This was short-sighted. For the Treaty to remain effective, virtually all the non-nuclear states must believe that the regime serves their country's long-term interests; and a significant majority must see the terms of the Treaty as being fair. Fairness is important because its correlate – resentment – is a powerful and corrosive motivator.

Meanwhile, the tacit pledge that the nuclear-weapon states would do all in their powers to avoid the resort to nuclear weapons has been replaced by the normalization of such weapons. The US talks about using them in response to biological and chemical attack and is developing small warheads that can be used more readily (useable nukes). Britain and France, no longer constrained by fears of precipitating a nuclear exchange, talk in general terms of sub-strategic systems. It is politically significant that the NATO nuclear-weapon states seem disinclined to heed the concerns of the non-nuclear states. This contributes to the post-9/11 image of the 'the West against the Rest', a corrosive conception that is reinforced by the rhetoric of the Bush administration

I use the term 'NATO nuclear-weapon states' to differentiate the US, UK and France from Russia and China, because of their different approaches to nuclear weapons and war.[3] China delayed signing until 1992, seeing the Treaty as an attempt by the superpowers to perpetuate their nuclear duopoly. It only joined after the break-up of the Soviet Union. China favours the total elimination of nuclear weapons and has always had a declared policy of not being the first to use them.

The Soviets were, of course, co-signatories of the Treaty with America and Britain in 1968. In the mid-1970s, for sound strategic reasons, they adopted the doctrine of 'no first use'. At the beginning of 1986, having 'looked down the nuclear abyss' as they put it (i.e., faced up to very real danger of inadvertent war during the Reagan administration), the Soviets proposed the elimination of all nuclear weapons. Later that year, Gorbachev almost achieved agreement on this at the Reykjavik summit.

Both 'no first use' and nuclear elimination remained declared Russian policy until 1993, when plans for NATO enlargement into Eastern Europe became generally known. The NATO nuclear-weapon states specifically reject the doctrine of 'no first use' and in May 2004 John Bolton (then Assistant Secretary of State for Disarmament) made it clear that he saw negotiations on the elimination of nuclear weapons as a waste of time, as well as diverting attention from more important (if unspecified) issues.[4]

Besides the three NATO nuclear-weapons states, there is also NATO-in-Europe, which has a distinct political–military personality, and a nuclear one at that. Nuclear forces based in Europe are said to be 'essential to preserve the peace', US weapons are deployed in six of NATO's non-nuclear states, and NATO (read US) has specifically reserved the right to deploy nuclear weapons on the territory of new and future members of the alliance.

Western perceptions of NATO tend towards the image of a peaceable (and somewhat toothless) guard dog that no right-thinking person could object to. For others, NATO is an American-led military alliance, which can be (and to some extent has been) used to support what are essentially US policies. NATO has now extended its formal boundaries to the borders of the former Soviet Union (and beyond, in the case of the Baltic states), and NATO units are currently deployed in Afghanistan. NATO's insistence on the right to deploy nuclear weapons on the territory of new members is the antithesis of the 'exclusion' principle underlying the concept of nuclear-weapons-free zones. It does, however, explain why NATO resisted formalizing the *de facto* Nuclear Weapon Free Zone encompassing central Europe from the Arctic to the Black Sea. This would have interfered with plans to extend NATO eastwards. Reverse reasoning would explain why Washington supports the formation of a Nuclear Weapons Free Zone in Central Asia.

A cynical view is that whatever the original intentions, the Non-Proliferation Treaty is now a convenient instrument of US foreign policy. In terms of global power projection, it ensures that US conventional forces will not be deterred or hampered by the threat of a nuclear response, while the treaty can be used to justify punitive action against any 'rogue state' that is thought to be seeking such a capability. Regional Nuclear Weapons Free Zones have put large areas of the world 'in balk', while leaving the US a free hand in the areas of geopolitical concern. This cynical perception is doubly unfortunate because it tends to conflate dissatisfaction over the implementation of the Treaty with the wider dissatisfactions arising from the rich/poor and North/South divides, from the socio-economic circumstances that nourished al-Qaeda and similar movements, and from the polarizing effect of Bush's 'war on terrorism', with its simplistic slogan that 'you are either with us or against us'.

These different dissatisfactions each have their own fault lines, but it is an uncomfortable fact that in all cases, the NATO nuclear weapon states find themselves on one side and the 'dissatisfied' on the other. In other words, the Treaty is failing the test of being seen as fair. More important, increasing numbers of states are beginning to question whether the treaty still serves their long-term national interests. The so-called 'Swedish Rule' has been supplanted by the Indian General's dictum that the lesson of the Gulf War was that if you intend to tangle with America, you need a nuclear capability; a lesson that seemed to be borne out by the different treatment accorded Iraq and North Korea. The correlation between nuclear status and political influence is seen to be increasing and the mix of motivations to 'go nuclear' can include powerful drives like disenchantment, resentment and the need for respect, as well as the more tangible realities of domestic politics, as was the case in India.

This outline only gives a taste of the problems facing the Treaty and has not addressed the question of how America would react if the Treaty began to unravel. Would it seek to arrest the process by pre-emptive prevention? It seems to be seeking the capability to strike at key production facilities. And since Washington believes that the problem lies with *who* possesses nuclear weapons and not with the weapons themselves, how are we to decide who fits into which category?

I would argue that the circumstances surrounding the Non-Proliferation Treaty today, and the likely consequences of that situation (and I have only glanced at the short term and have not mentioned the longer term) requires a fundamental response involving a major policy initiative. First, what needs to be done? As a minimum we need to:

1 Halt and reverse the trend towards proliferation.
2 Weaken the perceived connection between nuclear weapons

on the one hand, and political status and national security on the other.

3 Refrain from developing and introducing new nuclear weapons.

4 Reassert the nuclear taboo.

5 Initiate a process leading to the elimination of nuclear weapons.

6 Develop policies to counter the image of 'The West versus the Rest' and the reality of 'unfairness' and 'double standards'.

7 Devise a political process and structure to accommodate threshold, virtual, declared and *de facto* nuclear states, as well as the five 'treaty' states.

Quite a list – and there is very little that Britain, while one of the NATO nuclear weapon states, can do about it. Which takes us right back to **opportunity costs** – the things Britain could do and achieve if it did not have a nuclear capacity. By the very fact of renouncing its nuclear capability, Britain would be furthering the goals I listed, meanwhile meeting the political requirement that we don't give up an asset without getting something in return. Britain would demonstrate the conviction that in our case (admittedly a special one), we did not consider nuclear weapons important to political status, nor were they necessary for national security. And as we know from our experience with the Biological and Chemical Warfare Conventions, our opinion would now be more persuasive, because no longer would we be urging 'Do as I say, not as I do.'

It is not pretended that a British decision to renounce nuclear weapons would affect the policies of existing nuclear-weapons states, or the decisions of states already determined for their own separate reasons to acquire such a capability. But such an initiative would represent a fresh throw of the dice, a shaking of the kaleidoscope, the opportunity for a new dispensation. This could be immensely important, opening up unexplored avenues and opportunities for fresh initiatives and new alliances in a field that is characterized by patronizing attitudes, entrenched positions, frustration, bad faith and distrust. We would also be in a position to argue publicly against the further development of nuclear weapons and emphatically reassert the nuclear taboo. And we are particularly well qualified to launch national and international programmes: first, to publicize the dangers inherent in nuclear weapons, the unavoidable risk of nuclear inadvertence, and the pernicious effect of nuclear arms racing on international relations; and second, to rectify some of the more misleading factual distortions used to justify the strategic arms race and to highlight the true costs of nuclear deterrence during the Cold War.

It so happens that of the eight nuclear-weapon states, only Britain has the option of renouncing its nuclear capability without jeopardizing what it sees as its 'supreme national interests'. I can imagine the cries of 'What about France?', but I am talking here about Britain. Given the wide consensus that we would not set out to acquire a nuclear capability if we didn't already possess one, and that we only retain it because, who knows, one day it might come in handy, and anyway, better safe than sorry . . . supreme national interests don't really come into the British picture. That is not true of France, which has a different history and a tightly argued national philosophy.

Moving on to the fifth item, Britain is uniquely qualified to 'initiate a process leading to the elimination of nuclear weapons', picking up where the Canberra Report left off in 1997, after its sponsor (the Australian Labour government) had lost a General Election focused on the economy.

To the objection that nothing can be done without Washington, recent examples argue otherwise: the Ottawa Convention on Land Mines; the International Criminal Court; the Kyoto Accords. Certainly, they are diminished by US non-participation, but all three represent positive developments in key aspects of international affairs. Another example is the UN Convention on the Third Law of the Sea (LOS III), which was strongly opposed in the early stages by the maritime powers (including the US and USSR), but after 15 years of negotiation was finally agreed in 1982. Although the US has yet to accede, it treats the Convention as customary international law. It is also relevant that, despite the US Senate refusing to ratify the Comprehensive Test Ban Treaty until 1999, dismissing it as 'a flawed approach to reducing threats to the international system', existing plans to establish an international global verification regime went ahead. This includes an International Monitoring System comprising just under 340 detection/monitoring facilities world-wide, and an International Data Centre.

Turning to the sixth item, the demonstration that Britain took its obligations under Article 6 of the NPT seriously would be a step in the direction of fairness and away from double standards, which contribute to the damaging image of the 'West against the Rest'. Britain would be in a strong position to open up the opaque workings of the suppliers' cartel and other agreements buttressing the Non-Proliferation Treaty, perhaps expanding them to include 'non-contributing' members from the wider international community. To mitigate the impression of 'the West versus Rest', there is no organizational reason why these various functions and regulatory mechanics could not be brought together in a single international body.

This leads into the last item and the immensely complex questions of how to handle or react to the different categories of nuclear and potentially nuclear states; of who is a 'good' or a 'bad' state (and who decides) – and on the criteria whereby some states are allowed to produce their own enriched uranium and stockpiles of plutonium, while others are denied any kind of uranium enrichment facility. The decisions and the way they are made are significant factors in the widespread sense of unfairness and double standards, and the image of an increasingly divided world.

If Britain renounced its nuclear capability, it would automatically assume a crucial *role* in discussions and negotiations on what needs to be done and what (if any) decision-making structure would be required. Britain's initiative would open up fundamentally new ways of thinking about the problem. This leads naturally to the opportunity costs of our nuclear capability in terms of **Britain's role in the world**. A country's role ultimately defines the national interests that need protecting or promoting (the basis of foreign policy) and the parameters of its security concerns (the basis of defence policy).

It is surprising that Britain's role was not discussed in the 1998 'foreign policy led' Strategic Defence Review; nor had it been properly discussed earlier. After the Falklands, grateful for Sidewinders and satellite imagery, Britain focused on the role of compliant ally. Since 1991, Britain has been seen as a spear carrier for *Pax Americana*, a role it adopted without public debate or consideration of alternatives.

Going back to the 1950s, in the wake of Suez we embraced the reassuring image of Britain as the influential hub of a three-circle Venn diagram comprising Europe, America and the Commonwealth. We might have lost an empire, but not our urge to advise and lead.

Earlier, in 1952, London had joined Washington in pressuring France to join a rearmed West Germany in the six-nation European Defence Community. We of course had larger fish to fry. Through today, we persist with our delusions of grandeur, epitomized in our self-appointed role as America's closest ally and our empty claim to provide a bridge across the Atlantic. They are reflected in the boasts made by Douglas Hurd and by Jack Straw that Britain was 'punching above its weight'. Like our nuclear capability, this urge to be up with the bigger boys has opportunity costs, for example the opportunity to be a fully committed member of the European Union, and the opportunity to throw what weight we do have behind the work of the so-called Middle Powers, whose international influence is related to their intellectual and moral authority as much as their military and economic capabilities.

In both these areas, Britain has a great deal to offer. And as – for a change – we would be driving, rather than riding pillion, our influence could be considerable.

In this discussion I have deliberately avoided the larger question of the ultimate elimination of all nuclear weapons, because that complex issue can be used to divert attention from this straightforward question affecting Britain's national interests, which requires no international negotiations.

I have already warned against being drawn into the logistics of Trident replacement (toys for the boys). We are addressing the prior question: '**Does Britain need a nuclear capability?**' There is a political window of opportunity, and the answer is either 'Yes' or 'No', depending on the calculus of costs and benefits. It does *not* depend on timetabling or lead times.

Finally, if Britain is to reap the political benefits of renouncing its nuclear capability, it has to be a clear-cut decision to go the whole way with an irreversible programme of action. Do not confuse it with disarmament or arms control, which can be done progressively or in stages. Putting warheads into storage will not do the trick. In this case there are no half-measures – you can't be just a little bit pregnant, it is either all or nothing.

# 8 Britain and the Bomb

## TIM GARDEN

### A time of uncertainty

We have moved into a somewhat confused period for Western policy on countering the threats from nuclear weapons. We look back on the period of the Cold War almost with nostalgia where the mixture of deterrence, confidence building and arms control appeared to offer an intellectually coherent approach to a very dangerous strategic situation. Proliferation was constrained, and much slower than many had predicted. For the decade of the 1990s, the nuclear threat seemed to sink beneath the waves of the more exciting challenges of peace support doctrine, and we looked for ways to reduce our own nuclear arsenals in a managed manner. However, the new century has brought a savage downturn to our perspective on future peace and security. The mass killing on 11 September 2001 has made the previously theoretical risks of non-state actors acquiring nuclear capabilities appear much more realistic. It has also given the United States administration much greater domestic support for a proactive security agenda, which includes addressing perceived risks from future proliferation. Revelations about the activities of A. Q. Khan, who disseminated nuclear technology to a number of clients, have further strengthened concerns. The illusory weapons of mass destruction, which were used to justify the 2003 intervention in Iraq, do not seem to have diminished the Anglo-Saxon world's enthusiasm for talking tough.

Yet, it is difficult today for a medium-sized democratic nuclear power, the United Kingdom, to articulate the purpose of its nuclear capability. The development, at extraordinary cost, in the aftermath of the Second World War of strategic nuclear forces, was understandable in terms of Britain's view of itself as a victorious world power. In the days of the Cold War, there was an intellectual argument for the enhanced deterrence that came from the UK as a second centre of nuclear decision-making. While the Soviet Union might have come to believe that the US would be unwilling to risk a strategic nuclear exchange on behalf of Europe, the presence of British, French and NATO weapons made such an assessment much less likely. With the end of the Cold War, the Warsaw Pact was dissolved. Former enemies have joined NATO and the EU. Russia has established close relations with NATO, and is no longer seen as having territorial ambitions.

There are currently no nuclear weapon states which threaten the United Kingdom. Thus the UK minimum deterrent force of four Trident submarines has no enemy to deter. Nevertheless, a decision to abandon the UK's nuclear weapon status cannot be made purely on the basis of normal threat analysis. It would be extremely unlikely that such a decision could be reversed if circumstances changed. Therefore a careful assessment of costs and benefits to UK security needs to be made before such an irrevocable step is taken. This chapter analyses the key issues of future threats, resource implications, international status, arms control and options for the future. It assumes that nuclear weapons can have no other purpose for the United Kingdom than as a deterrent. The taboo on their use for war-fighting has strengthened over the years since 1945, and must be maintained.

## Nuclear threats

When we look at the nuclear problem, we find that it remains limited in scope. The states with a known nuclear weapon capability are in alphabetical order: China, France, India, Israel, Pakistan, Russia, UK and US. Somewhat strangely, current Western policy seems to accept all of these as being to a greater or lesser extent all right. Counter-proliferation policy is not really directed at any of the eight in a serious way. North Korea claims to have a nuclear capability, which if true is rudimentary. Yet some of these capabilities affect regional stability. Israel would argue that its nuclear weapons provide a deterrent against attack by weapons of mass destruction or overwhelming conventional force in an area with virtually no strategic depth. Its Arab neighbours are concerned to be threatened by nuclear capability without their own ability to deter. This gives a strategic rationale for Iraq, Iran, Syria, Saudi Arabia and Egypt to pursue such capabilities. Similarly, we can see the concerns raised by the India–Pakistan–China nuclear weaponry on each other, and on neighbours. A North Korean nuclear capability has implications for not just South Korea, but also for Japan and beyond. A longer term policy aim must be to reduce this dependence on nuclear and weapons of mass destruction capability.

In terms of missile delivery systems, the nations either operating or developing capabilities for missiles of over 500 km range are: the five nuclear weapon states, plus India, Iran, Iraq, Israel, North Korea, Libya, Pakistan, Saudi Arabia, Syria and Taiwan. All of the proliferators are in reaction to regional rather than global balances of power, although gaining a nuclear capability would change their status within the international community. Iran is active in its development of both cruise and ballistic missiles. Libya has tried unsuccessfully to obtain strategic missile technology, but has now opened up to inspection and co-operation. We have also become more aware of how a policy of isolating proliferators can make them sell on their technology. Following the Iraq regime change of 2003, the focus for international attention has been on Iran and North Korea.

While the state-to-state problem of weapons of mass destruction remains, the more difficult problem is that of non-state actors. The West possibly faces three different types of security threats: al-Qaeda type fanatical terrorists; terrorists furthering a regional power agenda, and perhaps insurgents taking operations back to the occupying forces' homeland. None of these is very likely to have a nuclear explosive capability, but all could be prepared to use it if they gained one. In this, the stability of Pakistan is a particular concern, as well as the long-known problem of nuclear material in post-Soviet Russia. None of the potential terrorist users are likely to be deterred by counter-threats. The most effective methods to be adopted will be the traditional counter-terrorist intelligence, police and protective measures.

## UK nuclear policy

Since the end of the Cold War, the UK has taken all of its nuclear weapons out of service apart from the remaining Trident ballistic missile systems based on four submarines. After the Strategic Defence Review of 1998, even the numbers of those missiles and warheads per missile were further reduced. UK nuclear forces now number four submarines, each with a maximum of 16 missiles carrying a maximum total of 48 warheads in one submarine. The total warhead stockpile is under 200, which makes the UK the smallest of the five official nuclear weapon states, and it may even have fewer than Israel. Nevertheless, 48 nuclear weapons represents a devastating power. The Review recognized that this could be inappropriate and hence incredible. It said therefore:

The credibility of deterrence also depends on retaining an option for a limited strike that would not automatically lead to a full scale nuclear exchange. Unlike Polaris and Chevaline, Trident must also be capable of performing this 'sub-strategic' role.

What was not explained in any more detail was the thinking behind this sub-strategic task. Presumably it was for occasions when one or two nuclear weapons might be sufficient to show resolve in some unspecified future crisis. However, the Review was quite clear on the circumstances under which UK nuclear weapons could and could not be used. It repeated what is known as the Negative Security Assurance, and spelled out what that assurance means:

> Britain has repeatedly made it clear that we will not use nuclear weapons against a non-nuclear weapon state not in material breach of its nuclear non-proliferation obligations, unless it attacks us, our Allies or a state to which we have a security commitment, in association or alliance with a nuclear weapon state. Britain has also undertaken to seek immediate UN Security Council action to assist any non-nuclear-weapon state party to the Non-Proliferation Treaty that is attacked or threatened with nuclear weapons.

This assurance is designed to act as an encouragement to non-nuclear weapon states to stay that way, and is a sensible diplomatic approach to dissuade potential proliferators. That said, like any assurance given in peaceful times, it will probably not be believed by an enemy at times of crisis. Thus Saddam Hussein may have been deterred from using chemical weapons during the first Gulf War, because he believed that there was a possibility of Western nuclear retaliation. Deterrence can happen without explicit statements.

## Beyond Trident

The British government has indicated that it needs to consider relatively soon what to do about the nuclear deterrent capability in anticipation that the current system will need replacement. It has not been clear on why a decision is needed so early. The original decision on the Trident programme was announced on 15 July 1980 and the first boat was operational in 1994 with a planned life of 30 years. Trident D5 itself was an overly sophisticated procurement, but at the height of the Cold War was seen as a good 'off-the-shelf' deal with the US. By the time it came into service, the Cold War was over, and a much less complex system would have sufficed. If any successor system were to take as long, a decision would be needed in 2010 for the first replacement in 2024. This could be extended by the phased changeover as the fourth Trident submarine does not go out of service until 2029.

Most weapon systems are kept in service for far longer than originally planned. They receive mid-life extensions to keep them viable. They may change their method of operating in later life to further extend their time in service. Nuclear systems are no different, and it might be expected that Trident could be operated well beyond the current expected out-of-service dates. There are no defences in prospect that would reduce its deterrent effect. Thus one option is continuation of the current minimum deterrent force for the indefinite future, with life extension work when necessary. Given the lack of any enemy with advanced counter-measures, it is possible that the Trident system could be operated on more constrained deployments if necessary.

## The strategic rationale

Now state-based threats are much reduced, it is difficult to outline a convincing scenario in which the UK deterrent plays a key part. However, we have seen very great changes in the international security situation over the past two decades. Looking forward over a similar period, we cannot discount equally dramatic upheavals. On current plans, a replacement system would have to counter possible challenges in the period 2025 to 2055. We have no crystal ball to tell us whether the threats will be from undeterrable non-state actors, or from a return to nationalism with nuclear-armed potential enemies. Nor can we know if the world will have become more peaceful, and nuclear weapons a historic irrelevance. This uncertainty underpins the strategic rationale for continuing to deploy a nuclear weapons capability. By the middle of the century, the international power structures could have changed markedly, and our successors might regret a decision taken now, which deprived them of a deterrent option, or had committed them to a system which had no relevance to the circumstances of the day.

Some would claim a further strategic justification beyond the defence rationale. They argue that Britain's place in the world is in part related to its nuclear status. While such arguments may have had some credibility in the immediate post-Second World War period, economic strength has become a more important factor in the age of globalization. In any future reform of the United Nations, membership of the Security Council will not be decided on the basis of nuclear weapon ownership. Only in the field of arms control will nuclear status continue to offer a special status at international negotiations.

A more compelling foreign policy rationale for retaining the minimum deterrent force is that it gives the UK a significant card to play in future nuclear disarmament negotiations. All the nuclear powers have undertaken commitments under the Non-Proliferation Treaty progressively to reduce their nuclear arsenals. The UK retains some leverage on this process while it has some weapons.

## The costs of nuclear status

In any analysis of future defence capability, the question of costs must be a major consideration. Acquisition of Trident cost £12.52 billion at 1998 prices, while current running costs are around £700 million per year. Just as Trident procurement was described in 1982 as being comparable to the Tornado acquistion, we might expect a successor system to bear comparison with Typhoon or aircraft carrier procurement costs. Some argue that the next generation of nuclear weapons may be designed to be smaller and carried by cruise missiles. These missiles would replace similar conventional weapons on submarines, ships or aircraft. However, it is unlikely that any nuclear certified system can be procured cheaply. Design costs and safety requirements will drive costs up. There are also costs associated with the decommissioning of the current system. Disposal of nuclear-powered submarines and redundant warheads will be a significant cost to the defence budget. Changes to the planned dates for removal from service will have consequential effects on the defence programme. An early removal will cause extra unplanned expenditure; a delay will ease defence budget pressures.

A related, but separate, cost question will be whether the need for a particular system merits its share of the defence budget. The effect on other conventional capabilities – the opportunity costs – are likely to be considerable. The defence budget is under progressive strain through the tightening effect of greater than normal inflation. Military personnel and equipment costs rise at rates above that of domestic inflation. With budgets limited in real terms, this results in year-on-year cuts in the size of armed forces. Provision of a nuclear weapon system, which has no utility against virtually all security challenges, will use funds that would provide for tasks that armed forces are undertaking on a regular basis.

## What should we do?

To make the judgement on the way forward, the key issue is to seek which approach has the best prospect of providing, and if possible enhancing, long-term security for the UK. This requires an approach which will not adversely affect international security. The relatively low running costs of Trident, coupled with high decommissioning costs, mean that there is no strong rationale for taking it out of service early, unless that could be shown to provide plausible security benefits. Maintenance of the current minimum deterrent posture does not stimulate proliferation, or carry any significant risks of accidental use. If some future international arms control opportunity arose, where we could improve our security by reducing or eliminating our nuclear weapons, then it would be a different calculation. Such a possibility does not look likely currently, but over the next two decades there may be new initiatives. If global reductions in nuclear weapons could be achieved through the UK putting its capability on the negotiating table, then security could be enhanced.

Any radically new nuclear system, whether ballistic or cruise missile based, would involve significant development costs for the platform, missile and warhead. Such costs would put further pressure on a defence budget which is already finding it difficult to retain coherence. Nor is it clear that such systems could contribute to our security needs beyond deterring indeterminate future nuclear threats. The constraints of the Non-Proliferation Treaty would cause further complications.

If Trident becomes limited in its capability through age, then using it in a more constrained mode can be considered. The need for long underwater patrols was a requirement of the Cold War, when second strike survivability was the key deterrence factor. Indeed, there will be many decision points in the years ahead about how much to invest in extending the life of the Trident system. A sustained improvement in the international security situation might allow for storage of weapons separate from the missiles at some future date, with the submarines maintained in dock on a care and maintenance basis.

It is clear that the prudent way forward today is to keep the Trident system going with life extension programmes, when needed. We can have a useful public debate about the future of UK nuclear weapons, but we would be foolish to rush into decisions that are likely to prove costly and irrelevant.

# 9 Turning the Nuclear Periscope: A View from Over the Channel

## TOM SAUER

Every 30 years a major strategic decision has to be taken in the UK: whether (and how) to modernize its floating nuclear weapons arsenal or not. This time not only the British people but even outsiders are asked to comment.

The inherent laws of politics make me rather sceptical about the effect of the debate in the UK. In modern democracies the inner circle inside the Executive usually takes the crucial decisions, and probably rightly so. In this chapter, I will point out why I believe that the final decision will probably be in favour of modernization and against unilateral nuclear disarmament. At the same time, I will argue why modernization would be the wrong decision, both from a national and global point of view. Throughout the chapter I will try to de-mythologize what in my eyes should be de-mythologized.

### A decision in the offing

Fundamental changes in politics only happen in case of overwhelming objective causes and in case of political leadership, i.e. statesmanship. Most of the time, however, politics correspond to what Charles Lindblom called 'incrementalism' or 'muddling through', adapting policy to the changed circumstances in a piecemeal fashion.[1] This characteristic of politics applies especially to policy that is perceived as having been

successful in the past. To explain this habit, political psychology is of particular use. Tversky and Kahneman have developed a theory – prospect theory – that states that people are
risk-prone when they can lose a lot and risk-averse when they
can win a lot.[2] Political scientists have used prospect theory to
show that political decision-makers in all likelihood prefer not
to take big risks, for instance by changing policy fundamentally
in order to win something, i.e. the estimated positive effects
of the proposed policy change. Prospect theory predicts that
decision-makers prefer a *status quo*, especially in cases in which
the overall benefits of the policy change are only expected in the
medium or long term.[3] One of the reasons is that there is an
imbalance between the public reaction of the opponents and the
advocates of fundamental policy change. Some (small) con-
stituencies will be immediately negatively affected by a radical
policy change and will do everything they can to prevent the
decision, for instance by making their grievances public. They
will also remember the issue at the ballot box. All this may
undermine the chances of the decision-maker to be re-elected,
which is in the end the core business of politicians. On the other
hand, the beneficiaries of change – who in case of fundamental
policy change will usually outnumber the opponents – will not
feel the necessity to speak out as much as the opponents, partly
because they expect decision-makers to make them better off.[4]
Furthermore, the chance is small that that particular issue will
determine their voting behaviour.

To halt the UK's nuclear weapons programme would signify
a fundamental policy change. Since 1952, UK's defence policy
relies on a nuclear deterrent. Most people in Britain have not
known it differently. They are used to it, maybe even addicted.
They have been told every now and then that it was due to
nuclear weapons that no Third World War has taken place.
Most people – especially the elder generation who have experienced the Second World War at first hand – regard nuclear
weapons with a positive connotation. According to an opinion

poll in the second half of the 1990s, 70 per cent of the British public wanted to keep the British nuclear weapons in 'all' or 'some' circumstances.[5] According to this logic, nuclear weapons have made the crucial difference during the Cold War.

This belief in the quasi-automatic stability of nuclear deterrence is a first myth. More to the point, nobody knows which factor was (most) responsible for the so-called 'long peace'. First of all, the concept of 'long peace' in itself is questionable. Millions of people have died during the Cold War as the superpowers exported their conflicts to the periphery through the so-called proxy wars. The Cold War was also the period in which the current 'war on terror' finds its origins. Second, and more fundamentally, there have been other factors that explain the absence of another world war: the memory of the former world wars in which more than 50 million people died; the reconciliation of the two hereditary enemies France and Germany thanks to the establishment of the European Coal and Steel Community, which became the European Community and later the European Union; the Atlantic Alliance as both a collective defence organization and security community; and the economic progress after 1945 ('Make trade not war'). This is not to claim that nuclear weapons did not play a role at all. The point is that the odds are that there are other and probably more important reasons for explaining the absence of another world war than the existence of nuclear weapons.

Further, the stability theory cannot always be backed up by empirical analysis. First of all, the world after 1945 came very close to global catastrophe despite the growing nuclear arsenals on both sides of the ocean. Recently opened archives have shown that the Executive Committee, the group of 'wise men' that President Kennedy had assembled to manage the Cuban missile crisis in October 1962, was not even aware that there were nuclear weapons on the island during the crisis, and that military officers had been ordered to use them in case of an American attack. At the same time, a majority of Kennedy's advisers was in favour of a preventive attack on different occasions during the 13-day meeting of the Executive Committee. If President Kennedy had listened to the hawks, the world might have looked very different.

Second, in the past, the stability resulting from nuclear weapons was not automatically generated. I do not have to remind the British audience of failures of nuclear deterrence, i.e. cases in which non-nuclear weapon states attacked nuclear weapon states, knowing very well that the latter could have retaliated with nuclear weapons. That is exactly what happened when Argentina invaded the Falklands in the beginning of the 1980s. The argument that the Falklands did not belong to the core territory of the UK and therefore did not belong to the British vital interests is undermined by the British reaction at that time. An even clearer example of a nuclear weapon state whose core territory has been attacked is Israel in 1973. Egypt and Syria were at that time very much aware that Israel possessed a screwdriver nuclear weapons option. Again, nuclear deterrence failed. A last example of failure of nuclear deterrence is the 1991 Gulf War. The US threatened at that time to use nuclear weapons if Saddam Hussein had used chemical or biological weapons, *or* sought to burn the oilfields. He did not use weapons of mass destruction (at that time), but he did burn the oilfields. In addition, he launched missiles against Israel, which is another nuclear weapon state. As a result, nuclear deterrence did not work in this case either.

These examples show the inherent difficulty related to nuclear deterrence, namely its credibility. The destructive power of atomic weapons is such that it is hard to come up with realistic scenarios in which political decision-makers in the twenty-first century will even think about using them again. The erosion of the credibility of nuclear deterrence grew during the second half of the twentieth century because of two reasons. First of all, the '*ius in bello*', and more particularly the norm of proportionality in war-fighting, gradually became further established and respected. Second, every single day without the use of nuclear weapons strengthened the nuclear taboo. There have been many occasions in which nuclear weapons in theory could have been used (like Vietnam). Political decision-makers – both in democracies and autocracies – always found a reason not to use them.

The only conclusion that can be drawn from this empirical record is that the military usefulness of nuclear weapons is practically non-existent. The first politician who will dare to use nuclear weapons again will provoke immense reactions from worldwide opinion, the extent of which cannot even be imagined. As a result, nobody believes that nuclear weapons will be used again.[6] The fact that everybody is aware of this dilemma is problematic for the nuclear weapon states. Consequently, nuclear threats become more and more hollow. What Galtieri, Saddam Hussein and Nasser did was therefore not irrational. They made an educated (and correct) guess that the nuclear threats of respectively the UK, the US and Israel were not credible. Not one of these countries did use nuclear weapons despite their implicit or explicit threat. In the end, their policy of nuclear deterrence became even further undermined.

Despite these limitations, nuclear weapons were generally accepted during the Cold War by both the foreign policy establishment and the public at large, at least in the nuclear weapon states. On the other hand, there have always been outspoken critics. Scientists like Joseph Rotblat, who later on would receive the Nobel Peace Prize, quit the Manhattan Project once Hitler was defeated. He did not agree with the use of nuclear weapons against Japan. His boss Oppenheimer unsuccessfully spoke out against the construction of the H-bomb at the end of the 1940s. A couple of years later, the Einstein–Russell manifesto criticized the ongoing atomic arms race.

The anti-nuclear peace movement originated from the large-scale nuclear tests, which became forbidden in 1963 with the

Partial Test Ban Treaty. The peace movement was resurrected in Western Europe at the end of the 1970s as a result of the so-called dual track decision by NATO with respect to the installation of the American Pershing II intermediate range nuclear missiles in the region. Despite massive protests both in Europe and the US, political decision-makers did not yield to the anti-nuclear rallies, at least not in public. A schism was established between the foreign policy elite and the progressive wing of public opinion, even within the nuclear weapon states, including the UK.

## The end of the Cold War

Today, even part of the foreign policy establishment is clearly in favour of eliminating nuclear weapons. Since the end of the 1980s, we live in a completely different world. First of all, the enemy against which the British (and American and French) nuclear weapons were targeted does not even exist any more. The USSR is no more. While Russia has not (yet) become a full democracy, the difference between the current regime and the Soviet regime is significant. Russia is a partner that belongs to the G-8. Russian military walk around in NATO's headquarters. The UK is not a target any more for Russia, and vice versa.

Second, bipolarity has been replaced by a mixture of multi-polarity and unipolarity. Those who believed in the nuclear balance of terror between the USSR and the US cannot automatically assume that a world with more centres and with more nuclear weapon states (including for instance India and Pakistan) will result in a similar level of stability. Only hard-core deterrence theorists do not look to the type of regime and assume that all states are rational players and therefore can be deterred. In the real world, most experts, including government officials of the nuclear weapon states, doubt whether so-called rogue states like Iran and North Korea (and Pakistan) are to the same extent deterrable. A report of the British Ministry of Defence of December 2002 made that clear: 'We must . . . take very seriously the danger that deterrence will be less effective against new owners of these awesome capabilities who may not subscribe to international norms of behaviour and may be willing to take greater risks than were the leaders of the Soviet Union.'[7]

Many (retired) politicians, diplomats, generals and scientists who had been involved at the highest levels of nuclear decision-making during the Cold War changed from being pro-nuclear to being anti-nuclear after the fall of the Berlin Wall. Some of them became the most outspoken voices in favour of nuclear elimination. Examples are Robert McNamara (former US Secretary of Defence under Kennedy and Johnson), General Lee Butler (former US Chief of the Strategic Air Command at the end of the 1980s and beginning of the 1990s) and Paul Nitze (US Chief Nuclear Arms Control Negotiator in the 1980s). In the UK, Joseph Rotblat was joined by former Prime Minister James Callaghan, former Secretary of Defence Lord Denis Healey, retired generals Lord Michael Carver (British Chief of Defence, 1973–76) and Sir Hugh Beach[8], and academics such as Ken Booth[9] and Michael MccGwire[10] (both from the University of Aberystwyth), Robert O'Neill (Oxford University and member of the Canberra Commission) and Michael Clarke (King's College)[11]. Different studies and reports were published in the 1990s, calling for minimum deterrence and even nuclear elimination. The most famous report is the Canberra Commission Report (1996). The initiative to bring together a group of 'wise men' from all over the world to think about the future of nuclear weapons came from Australia in the wake of the regional uproar after the French nuclear tests.

Even some high-level officials inside the nuclear weapon states thought through the consequences of the end of the Cold War and spoke out *before* they retired. Clinton's first Secretary of Defence Les Aspin, for instance, concluded that the costs of nuclear weapons, especially the spread of nukes over more and more countries, outweighed their benefits. He repeated on different occasions that nuclear weapons were the big equalizer and therefore not in the interest of the hegemon.

Still others became convinced of the desirability of a nuclear-weapons-free world after the terrorist attacks on 11 September 2001. For the first time ever, nuclear terrorism became a danger that could not be ignored any more.[12] Also IAEA Director General Mohamed El Baradei – who received the Nobel Peace Prize in December 2005 – became a vocal advocate of thinking out of the box, namely beyond nuclear deterrence. In a speech for Swedish students in December 2005, he said 'to continue to have the 'haves' and 'have-nots' is absolutely unsustainable' and that this world is 'in denial'.[13] But also somebody like former UK Minister of Defence Michael Portillo (from the Conservative Party) is nowadays an opponent of the modernization of the British nuclear deterrent.[14]

## Lack of political leadership and nuclear inertia

But, as argued at the beginning, politics is rather complex. Despite all objective reasons to get rid of nuclear weapons and despite the fact that so many experienced and acknowledged experts who have been part of the foreign policy establishment in the past actively pleaded for such a policy change, nuclear weapons policy has *not* fundamentally changed over the last years: there are still 27,000 nuclear weapons on earth, the Cold War force structure, and the declaratory and operational policies of the nuclear weapon states are basically kept in place.

The reason why this is so can be derived from the political model described above: bureaucratic resistance and lack of political leadership. A tiny minority of people that is personally affected by a policy change, namely those who work in the nuclear weapons complex, either as engineers or scientists in the nuclear weapons labs (like Aldermaston), or as civilian or military officials dealing with nuclear weapons policy in the Ministry of Defence, will do everything they can to resist the policy change. It is no surprise to find out that they are in favour of modernization of the British nuclear submarines, missiles and warheads. Their careers depend for a large part on that decision. If these weapon systems are not modernized, they will have to find other jobs. By different subtle tactics, these officials can make life hard for their superiors in the administration who are willing to change course, let alone for the politicians. It should be stressed that we are talking about a very tiny minority of the British people: 3,000 scientists and a couple of hundred military and officials from the Ministry of Defence.[15] A majority of the officer corps would vote against diverting the defence budget into another generation of non-usable nuclear weapons.[16]

This is exactly what happened during the first major nuclear policy review after the Cold War in the US. The Clinton administration, and in particular Secretary of Defence Les Aspin, wanted to adapt US nuclear weapons policy to the radically changed circumstances. Les Aspin and his Assistant Secretary of Defence in charge of strategic nuclear weapons policy, Ashton Carter, issued the Nuclear Posture Review in the autumn of 1993. But to their surprise, the working groups of the Review that were staffed with mid-level military (colonels) and civilian officials, did *not* come up with new options. These mid-level officials succeeded in blocking any major or even minor reform. Robert McNamara called the outcome of the Review one year later 'an absolute disgrace'.[17]

Again, the reason was gigantic bureaucratic resistance and a lack of political leadership. Three months after the start of the Nuclear Posture Review, Secretary of Defence Les Aspin had to resign because of the Somalia disaster. With President Clinton struggling with the military starting from week one in office, due to a difference of views about the rights of gays in the military, and no other senior political appointee willing to fight for the Review, Assistant Secretary of Defence Ashton Carter was left alone in his struggle with the bureaucracy. Despite his superior rank, he lost the bureaucratic game.[18]

During the Nuclear Posture Review, public opinion in the US did not play a role at all. The one thing that came closest to a societal debate was the invitation of a couple of experts from think-tanks like the Brookings Institute, to give a presentation in one of the working groups. These presentations were dismissed by the latter as 'too idealistic' and 'out of touch with reality'.

The crucial question becomes whether Prime Minister Tony Blair can and will do what Bill Clinton did not, namely stand up against the nuclear weapons establishment. Despite the changed circumstances and despite the promises in the 1998 Strategic Defence Review,[19] my personal assessment is that Blair will be afraid of rocking the boat as well. In principle, Blair – like Clinton – has the personality to push radical changes through and to convince public opinion of the rightness of the decision. But at the same time, both Clinton and Blair cling very much to the daily opinion polls and most of the time they do not show leadership. For instance, Blair did not announce that he would bring the UK into the Eurozone. Did he really try in the end? Further, Blair did not speak out against Bush while the rest of the world was convinced that it was wrong to invade Iraq. The 'principle' of remaining a close ally of the US prevailed above anything else. There is, however, nothing heroic about this bandwagoning strategy. Following the leader is exactly the opposite of leading.

Another parallel with Clinton is that both politicians led and lead a so-called left-wing party, which is by definition vulnerable in the field of defence policy. Rightly or wrongly, progressive parties are believed to be softer on these issues, something that resonates in public opinion. In theory, this is correct. In practice, many of these left-wing parties once in office do everything they can not to rock the boat with the foreign and defence policy establishment, knowing very well that they can easily be criticized for being soft. That is also the reason why Republican presidents in the US have better arms control credentials than their Democratic counterparts because the latter have more difficulty convincing military and public opinion.

In the UK, this kind of political psychology seems to be even stronger. There exists what I would call Labour's 'nuclear disarmament syndrome'. It is generally believed that Labour lost the elections in the 1980s because of its radical view on nuclear disarmament. Regardless of whether this is true, and I personally believe that it is another myth, the circumstances today are fundamentally different. Political scientists however have shown that using historical analogies wrongly is a common mistake of politicians.[20] There is a substantial risk that Tony Blair will do the same and will evade the choice in favour of unilateral nuclear disarmament. This decision will in large part be based on emotions that result from a negative experience in the past.

## Debunking other nuclear myths

Other arguments sometimes turn up in favour of keeping the existing policy. Some of these are taken for granted by small or large segments of public opinion. It is high time to debunk them too.

### 'Nuclear weapons states are allowed to possess nuclear weapons'

The cornerstone of the nuclear non-proliferation regime is the Nuclear Non-Proliferation Treaty that was signed in 1968. The Treaty acknowledged the existence of five nuclear weapon states: those who had exploded a nuclear device before 1 January 1967, namely the US, the USSR, the UK, France and China (in chronological order). Advocates of nuclear weapons sometimes forget that this discrimination was not meant to endure for ever. All other states had to sign up as non-nuclear weapon states. The deal was the following: the non-nuclear weapon states promised never to acquire nuclear weapons and to accept International Atomic Energy Agency inspections; in return, they were promised help with their civilian nuclear programmes (art. 4) and the nuclear weapon states promised to disarm their nuclear weapons in turn (art. 6).

Advocates of nuclear weapons argue that the language of art. 6 is rather vague. More particularly, they point out that the article does not talk about 'abolition' or 'elimination', but about 'nuclear disarmament', which in addition was linked to conventional disarmament.

At the 1995 Non-Proliferation Treaty Review and Extension Conference and at the 2000 Review Conference, all state parties, including the nuclear weapon states, however, agreed with language that left no ambiguity: it talks about 'nuclear elimination' *without* a link to conventional disarmament. One may point out that these agreements are, strictly speaking, not legally binding (treaty-based) commitments. That is correct, but not relevant as they are politically binding in the sense that the Treaty – 25 years after entering into force – had to be renewed in 1995. The non-nuclear weapon states only agreed to the indefinite extension of the Treaty on the condition of working out an action plan with respect to nuclear disarmament. If the nuclear weapon states, especially the US and France, nowadays backpedal with respect to this action plan, they are playing with the fate of the Treaty. That is at least the perception by the non-nuclear weapon states. The Brazilian diplomat Sergio Duarte, who would chair the 2005 Review Conference, warned the nuclear weapon states from the beginning: 'So, if every five years you accept a number of political commitments, and then five years later you say you no longer support those commitments or part of those commitments, the results for the international community is [sic] a very bad one.'[21]

To conclude, the nuclear weapon states (including the UK)

are not allowed to keep their nuclear weapons for ever. They are obliged to take steps to get rid of them. The longer the nuclear weapon states wait to make that happen, the more non-nuclear weapon states will – partly out of the combination of insecurity, imitation and frustration – acquire nuclear weapons as well, which may unravel the whole nuclear non-proliferation regime. As Robin Cook argued one week before his sudden death in the summer of 2005: 'There is a chasm too wide for logic to leap, between arguing that Britain must maintain nuclear weapons to guarantee its security, and lecturing Iran *et al* that the safety of the world would be compromised if they behaved in the same way.'[22]

## 'Nuclear weapons as a last resort against nuclear proliferation and nuclear terrorism'

'The continuing risk from the proliferation of nuclear weapons, and the certainty that a number of other countries will retain substantial nuclear arsenals, mean that our minimum nuclear deterrent capability, currently represented by Trident, is likely to remain a necessary element of our security',[23] states a UK MOD White Paper of December 2003.

To argue, however, that the nuclear weapon states need nuclear weapons to deter future proliferators is turning the logic upside down. Proliferators obtain nukes partly because of the existence of nuclear weapons. In other words, if there were no nuclear weapons on earth, the difficulty of acquiring them would be much bigger (due to the enhanced verification mechanisms) and the incentives for nuclear proliferation would be much smaller. To argue that one should keep nuclear deterrence against potential nuclear proliferators is more or less the same as arguing to keep nuclear weapons for ever. The latter is in contradiction with article 6 of the Non-Proliferation Treaty.

To use nuclear deterrence as an instrument against nuclear terrorism makes absolutely no sense because terrorists by definition cannot be deterred, i.e. targeted in the first place, and even if that were possible, al-Qaeda operatives are not afraid to die.

Both arguments are misused by those who have a parochial interest in keeping nuclear weapons.

### 'Nuclear weapons yield prestige'

Another advantage of nuclear weapons besides stability would be prestige, or at least that is how the argument goes.

Maybe that is true for the nuclear weapon states and part of their public opinion. But most non-nuclear weapon states, including their public opinion, have the opposite view. They do not like nuclear weapons. President Chirac for instance miscalculated the reaction in the rest of the world against the resumption of the French nuclear tests in the summer of 1995. Worldwide protests, including wine boycotts, led to a reappraisal of the French decision and to stop earlier than planned.

To give another example: the reason why the idea of a Euro-bomb is taboo has not only to do with the unwillingness of the UK and France to share the button, but even more because of the general anti-nuclear attitude in countries such as Germany, Belgium, the Netherlands, Ireland and Sweden. Consequently, if the UK were to become the first official nuclear weapon state that eliminates its nuclear weapon arsenal, it would gain standing and prestige in many countries around the world.

### 'Nuclear weapons are useful bargaining instruments'

This argument is a bit more subtle in the sense that it does not oppose getting rid of nuclear weapons, but only the UK doing it unilaterally. Ideally, all nuclear weapon states should join the UK and eliminate their arsenals as well. As some nuclear weapon states are situated in more unstable regions and/or possess many more nuclear weapons than the UK, it is unrealistic to assume that the others will follow the UK just because it suits the latter's agenda.

The only realistic way out is to start multilateral negotiations for a Nuclear Weapons Convention (like the Chemical Weapons Convention and the Biological Weapons Convention) that in its turn would set up the process of eliminating nuclear weapons worldwide. Until now, and in contrast to their legal obligations, the nuclear weapon states have been unwilling to start such negotiations. The question of modernizing the British arsenal or not presents an ideal opportunity for the UK to set up such a round of negotiations.

### 'Nuclear weapons cannot be destroyed'

Some people apparently believe that nuclear weapons cannot be dismantled. It is correct that it is not much easier to destroy than to build nuclear weapons, but the weapons can be dismantled. That process has been going on from the beginning of the 1970s. Some countries – like South Africa – have dismantled all their nuclear weapons. In this process, some choices have to be made, for instance what to do with the fissile material – plutonium and highly enriched uranium (HEU) – that result from the dismantlement. Exactly the same question, however, has to be answered in the civilian nuclear domain: HEU can be downblended to LEU, while plutonium can either be reprocessed via MOX or, even better, buried with a mixture of glass and other materials.

### 'Nuclear weapons cannot be disinvented'

It cannot be denied that the knowledge to build nuclear weapons cannot be disinvented. The knowledge exists. The genie cannot be put back into the bottle. On the other hand, people can un-learn habits. The world would have looked completely different if people had not had the capacity to learn from their own mistakes or, even better, from the mistakes of others. The same applies to states. At a certain period in time, people created the norm that slavery was inhumane and had to be abolished. Nowadays, slavery is abolished, even though it cannot be disinvented. A counter-argument is that in reality slavery still exists. While that is true, slavery remains illegal and punishable. Because it is relatively easy to cheat and because national authorities sometimes turn a blind eye, it still goes on. The latter is hardly possible in the case of nuclear weapons. In a nuclear weapons-free world, it will be extremely hard to cheat due to a very strict control regime. The latter may be feasible because each state has to take part in it.

## 'A nuclear weapons-free world will be more unstable'

Nuclear weapons create stability. Consequently, a nuclear weapons-free world will bring us back to the pre-1945 unstable world, the argument goes. As Michael Quinlan once stated: 'Better a world with nuclear weapons but no major war than one with major war but no nuclear weapons'.[24] But this logic does not make sense, for different reasons. First of all, it can be questioned whether nuclear weapons are really as stabilizing as commonly believed (see above). Second, the world has changed in the meantime. In contrast to the 1940s, the norm against inter-state war is nowadays generally accepted. There are more or less no inter-state wars any more because the international community has accepted the need to live in a world in which this rule applies and the few cheaters are sanctioned by the collective security system through the UN. This was, for instance, the case with Iraq after the invasion of Kuwait in 1990. Third, conventional weapons are an alternative. The use of modern conventional weapons may also inflict enormous damage and can therefore be used as a deterrent as well. The advantage of conventional weapons is twofold: first, to inflict the same degree of damage will take more time. This leaves scope for finding a political compromise and a break-up of the violence. Second, collateral damage is nearly absent in the case of conventional weapons. As Paul Nitze concluded in 1994: 'Smart conventional weapons are safer, cause less collateral damage, and pose less threat of causing escalation – therefore offering greater flexibility for use in situations where nuclear weapon use would be politically or militarily impractical'.[25] Michael Quinlan goes very far in the same direction by saying: 'America's massive non-nuclear military power could amply punish the perpetrators of a biological or chemical attack without resorting to nuclear weapons.'[26]

## 'In a nuclear weapons-free world, the nuclear cheater will dominate'

One of the so-called risks in a nuclear weapons-free world is that a state cheats and breaks out by secretly acquiring nuclear weapons. This is another myth. First of all, to reduce this risk, a moral/political climate must be created in which nuclear weapons are entirely de-legitimized. Second, and more fundamentally, it is far from clear what the absolute advantages are of possessing one or a few nuclear weapons in a nuclear weapons-free world. In the 'best' case – from the point of view of the offender – one can only briefly enjoy the potential benefits of its nuclear monopoly, while the rest of the world will restart building nuclear weapons. In the 'worst' case, the offender will be bombed to the pre-nuclear era and will be isolated for a very long time, while the rest of the world may possibly redeploy nuclear weapons. These scenarios do not look very attractive for potential cheaters.

## Conclusion

By deciding not to modernize its nuclear weapons arsenal, the UK may set a clear example for the other nuclear weapon states without undermining its own security. On the contrary, the UK may gain billions with which it can buy usable military instruments. As Michael MccGwire stated: 'Such an initiative would represent a fresh throw of the dice, a shaking of the kaleidoscope, the opportunity for a new dispensation.'[27] The other nuclear weapon states will be under huge pressure to follow. Even if that does not happen, it would have no negative security implications as the military value of nuclear weapons is nearly non-existent. On the contrary, the UK's reputation in the world will soar. The UK will be regarded as a soft power, something which has much more standing and prestige in today's interdependent trading world.

While this chapter argues that unilateral nuclear disarmament is desirable for the UK and the rest of the world, it also makes the case that it is not very likely, due to the inherent laws of politics and the lack of leadership qualities of British Prime Minister Tony Blair.

# 10  The Bomb is Not a Holy Weapon of Peace!

## TONY KEMPSTER

The birds they sang
at the break of day
Start again
I heard them say
Don't dwell on what
Has passed away
or what is yet to be.

The wars they will
be fought again
The holy dove
be caught again
bought and sold
and bought again
the dove is never free.

*Ring the bells that still can ring*
*Forget your perfect offering*
*There is a crack in everything*
*That's how the light gets in.*

We asked for signs
the signs were sent:
the birth betrayed
the marriage spent
the widowhood of every
    government –
signs for all to see.

Can't run no more
with the lawless crowd
while the killers in high places
say their prayers out loud.
But they've summoned up
a thundercloud
and they're going to hear from me.

You can add up the parts
but you won't have the sum
You can strike up the march,
there is no drum
Every heart
to love will come
but like a refugee.

*Ring the bells that still can ring . . .*

*Anthem* by Leonard Cohen (1992). Stranger Music Inc. The words were based on Kabbalistic sources, especially the writings of the sixteenth-century rabbi Isaac Luria.[1]

As a singer, I like to use the words of a popular or protest song as a background to discussion. Like art in its widest sense, such songs can contribute to an understanding of God replacing religious myths now deemed 'untrue' by scientific rationality. These words by the Canadian songwriter and poet, Leonard Cohen, will have been heard by hundreds of thousands of people and interpreted in different ways. Here they speak to the churches, to political leaders who may take nations to war in the future, and even to the pacifist with absolutist views.

To think seriously about nuclear weapons and their role in the future of humankind is impossible without a sense of foreboding – unless, like some New Evangelicals, one warmly anticipates 'a holy nuclear war' which will exalt Israel, crushing its enemies before going on to dramatize the Apocalypse.

This foreboding is captured in Martin Amis' *Einstein's Monsters*,[2] a title which he says refers not only to nuclear weapons but also to ourselves: 'We are Einstein's monsters: not fully human, not for now.' More than this, he suggests that nuclear weapons are mirrors in which we see all versions of the human shape, including the desire for God-like power.

Amis asks and answers: 'What is the only provocation that could bring about the use of nuclear weapons? – nuclear weapons. What is the only established defence against nuclear weapons? – by threatening to use nuclear weapons. How do we prevent the use of nuclear weapons? – by threatening to use nuclear weapons. And we cannot get rid of nuclear weapons, because of nuclear weapons.'

Perhaps this is why questions about the future of nuclear weapons are so disconcerting, knowing deep down as we do, that in the final analysis the alternatives are either nuclear war or nuclear disarmament. So we obfuscate and discuss the fine points of strategy, shying away from talk of abolition. Like the few remaining humans after the holocaust in the cult film, *Beneath the Planet of the Apes*,[3] we seem doomed to keep the 'bomb', revering it as a holy weapon of peace and, in the final human act, detonating it when threatened by the aliens (in the film's case, the apes who have taken over as the dominant species on Earth).

The 1988 report of the General Synod Board for Social Responsibility, *Peacemaking in a Nuclear Age*,[4] recognizes these concerns and sets out clearly the concept of Christian hope for a renewed world. It says:

> In a situation where many people are anxious and often fatalistic or cynical, the Church has a particular contribution to make concerning the long-term hope for the future. The philosophy of defence must be based on something more than an attempt to survive a process of confrontation and increasing arms procurement stretching into the future . . . The Christian view will also include a hope for the future dependent upon a theological understanding of history.

Such theological understanding is important and Church commitment to peace, spelt out in published reports, media statements and so on, very encouraging. But there is little to suggest that it has contributed to a serious and sustained opposition to militarism, of which nuclear weapons are a part. The spate of activity in peace-related institutions, education and research, that took place following the moral and physical exhaustion of the two world wars has gradually faded, affected particularly by the ending of the Cold War. Today, public awareness and resistance to militarism seem to be at a particularly low ebb.

Millions *did* march against the recent Iraq War, but this was a specific issue which was an affront to justice and democracy. By contrast, public meetings and demonstrations against the international arms trade (which fuels militarism), the US 'star wars' programme or the next generation of nuclear weapons rarely field more than a few hundred people. The Christian presence is mainly from the Quakers and denominational peace organizations which tend to be marginalized and linked weakly to the mainstream of the churches. It is also unfortunate that the

Churches Peace Forum, regarded by peace organizations as an important point of contact, has been wound up. This has left Churches Together in Britain and Ireland (CTBI) and the national ecumenical organizations without a specialist forum for discussion of urgent matters related to war and peace.

The general thrust of *The Church and the Bomb* report[5] was for more action. It concluded that 'Christians ought to relate the Churches' general teaching on war and peace to the circumstances of the present and have faith to come to specific conclusions, however provisional and imperfect they may seem to be.' Although not spelt out, the implication was surely that the Church itself should be more involved in peace education and projects to catalyze Christian resistance to militarism. (Note that this was not the view of the 1988 report *Peacemaking in a Nuclear Age*. Referring to Paul Ramsey's 1969 work, *Who Speaks for the Church?*,[6] it concluded in the same vein that the churches have a responsibility to deepen and broaden the discussion but not polarize the debate by finding in favour of a specific policy.)

The General Synod voted in 1983 to continue its support for Britain's nuclear arsenal. The decision was taken in full knowledge that the weapons were part of an open-ended arms race (with an implicit understanding that a first strike would be used if necessary), not a deterrent based on insights into the mutual motivations of NATO and the Soviet Union to prevent war.

But this was 20 years ago, when a commitment by any of the nuclear powers to abolish nuclear weapons lay largely outside the limits of mainstream discussion and well beyond the pale of political acceptability.

Times have changed with the ending of the Cold War, the emergence of international terrorism as a major threat and the new urgency of stopping further nuclear proliferation. Now, as the British government looks again at its nuclear capability, the Church could take an abolitionist position. Such a change would reassure people, particularly those of other faiths (many of whom still see the Church of England as a champion of militarism and even the Holy Crusade) and encourage them to listen and have greater faith in the Christian peace message. Furthermore, the Christian world is in need of a countervailing voice when one considers the stridency and growing influence of Evangelical Christians in US politics. These Christians, in seeking identity and assurances of security, are increasingly pre-disposed to elect politicians and embrace religious leaders who offer faith in the Bible and belief in God's word to protect them from harm.[7] For many of them, this equates with militarism and the early use of force to neutralize potential threats.

This seems a good time 'to start again and not dwell on what has passed away' as in the opening of *Anthem*.

## The special nature of nuclear weapons

It is common to regard nuclear weapons as unique and quite separate from other considerations of militarism. Use of the term 'nuclear pacifists', for those who would abolish nuclear weapons but continue to accept wars fought by other means is a reflection of this (and incidentally a misnomer since pacifists are by definition against all war as a way of settling inter-national disputes).

The alternative view is that nuclear weapons happen to be the latest class of weapons available, albeit the first weapons to have the potential to destroy humankind, and that war is the menace. As Joseph Rotblat, a scientist who worked on the first nuclear bomb and a committed abolitionist said: 'Even the elimination of nuclear weapons will not bring full security. Nuclear weapons cannot be disinvented and in a military con-frontation nations will be tempted to rebuild them . . . It is also already recognised that further research is likely to bring other means into being. In such circumstances, any war can threaten us, because any war can escalate without limit.'[8] In addition to his work for nuclear disarmament with Pugwash Conferences,

Jo was also founder president of Movement for the Abolition of War. With Robert Hinde, MAW's vice-president, he emphasized his point in *War No More, Eliminating Conflict in the Nuclear Age*[9] saying: 'In the nuclear age we simply cannot afford to have war, any war, because even a limited armed conflict could escalate into a nuclear holocaust.'

Thus, militarism has its own momentum, arms races leading to even more accurate, more cost-effective or more devastating weapons. This escalation often takes place as a result of fear and misunderstood motives, the response to one threat, often a defensive move, leading to another 'defensive move'. Reflecting on the Cold War, Robert McNamara wrote: 'The situation that we find ourselves in today has evolved over the years, through a series of incremental decisions without moral compass. Each of the decisions, taken by itself, appeared rational or inescapable . . . They have led to nuclear arsenals and nuclear war plans that few of the participants either anticipated or would, in retrospect, wish to support.'[10]

But today's concerns are more about the limited use of nuclear weapons than a major confrontation between nuclear powers. A war involving the selective use of nuclear weapons against an enemy that did not have them would not necessarily kill more people than a protracted war waged with conventional weapons. Some might even argue that the breaking of the nuclear taboo would be proportionate since it would bring a swifter victory with less loss of life.

Such a war might involve tactical nuclear weapons, a classification that is not formally regulated by any of the existing nuclear weapons treaties. These are the smaller weapons designed for battlefield use in the Cold War, but still capable of inflicting considerable damage. Because they are smaller, some experts fear that they are the most dangerous, as military officers may feel less constrained about using them in a desperate conflict situation. In its military posture review, the US has used the threat posed by rogue states, to increase the development of low-yield nuclear weapons that could even be used in cities.[11] This could be seen as a normalization of nuclear weapons as an integral part of defence policy, one which allows them to be placed on the soil of any ally and targeted against countries that may be considering or are even at the early stages of developing weapons of mass destruction. Another feature of the normalization of nuclear weapons has been the way both the US and UK governments have conflated in the public mind the different types of weapons of mass destruction, so that there is no distinction between a chemical battlefield weapon and the most destructive nuclear weapon.

### The dangers of militarism and preventative war?

The threat of military force is weakened as a foreign policy tool when the requirements for 'justifiable' use are closely regulated. For this reason, current US policy is seeking to shake off the constraints placed on its freedom of action by international agreements written and accepted during the last 20 years of the Cold War. Arms control agreements that might limit US freedom to defend itself are a focus, based on claims that they are too complex and compromise the deployment of military forces. This is dangerous ground because international law is notoriously flexible to interpretation and can be changed by action.

Of particular significance is the US view of pre-emptive war which blurs the edges with preventative war. Under the rules of international law there is space for pre-emption, when there is an immediate and necessary reason to respond to a threat, but preventative war might be based simply on the evaluation of a potential threat for the future. (Note that the potential use of nuclear weapons in this way undermines one of the basic precepts of the Non-Proliferation Treaty: that nuclear weapons states will not use or threaten to use nuclear weapons against non-nuclear weapons states that are members in good standing of the treaty.)[12]

Such flexibility, the US argues, is necessary to deal with the combination of terrorism and weapons of mass destruction, now seen as the greatest threat to security. And the UK government apparently accepts this since Geoff Hoon, the Secretary of State for Defence in the run-up to the Iraq wars insisted that Britain reserved the right to use nuclear weapons if Britain or its troops were threatened by chemical weapons.[13] In effect he was saying that the British Government would be willing to use a nuclear first strike against a non-nuclear state. (Note that this differs from NATO strategy which includes a potential first strike ('flexible response') implicitly against a nuclear state.)

The problem with a strategy involving pre-emption or preventative war is that it demands extraordinarily good intelligence when this cannot be guaranteed, as the lesson from the putative case for the Iraq War clearly demonstrates. Wrong targets, disastrous bombing, excessive collateral damage, regions in chaos are more credible outcomes than the power of intelligence to forestall them.

A more aggressive and militaristic US foreign policy is bound to encourage nuclear proliferation among those countries which feel threatened, as the history of nuclear weapons shows. Fear of a German bomb led to the US bomb and in sequence to the Soviet, Chinese, Indian and Pakistani bombs. As Schell points out: 'This series of threats and counter-threats forms an adamantine chain that links the leftover arsenals of the Cold War to the new arsenals springing up in the soil of South Asia.'[14]

## 'The price of peace' and the just-war doctrine

The way in which pre-emption is defined is a key factor in the Christian just-war doctrine. It has become an issue in 'The price of peace', a transatlantic dialogue between theologians, ethicists and legal experts set up by the Church of England and the Catholic Bishops' Conference of England and Wales, which will report later this year [2006]. I have discussed the implications of this elsewhere[15] and will simply reiterate the particular concern that a compromise with a US theological position (articulated particularly by George Weigel) might weaken the *jus ad bellum* criteria and the role of the UN in providing a mandate for military action. It is important that the churches hold a firm line on this.

## Pacifism and anti-militarism: definition and perspectives

So militarism is the menace, and nuclear weapons have to be dealt with in this context, a point made forcibly in the conclusion of *The Church and the Bomb*:

> We must emphasise once again, with the utmost force at our command, that nuclear weapons cannot be treated as an isolated issue, completely separable from the whole problem of war. They have simply brought forward the time when war in general is seen in all its futility as an alleged means of dealing with international or national disputes. War is no longer viable.[16]

This view of militarism underlies the pacifist position. Before examining this, we need to rehearse the meaning of pacifism to avoid misunderstanding.

While writing this chapter, I have been conscious of its singular place here among chapters by non-pacifist authors. I also feel favoured in that such a book of separate essays allows me to express the pacifist position without losing its thrust in consensual statements, as was the case for *The Church and the Bomb*. The working party, which included pacifist representation, was at pains to point out that its report was not pacifist, nor would it have been possible to agree on 'anything that could possibly be called such'. (Note that the group's decision to go beyond nuclear issues will almost certainly have contributed to this position.)

Then there is my personal position. As the title states: this is '*a* pacifist perspective': it does not speak for all pacifists or even a particular organization although I do hold to the pledge made by other members of the Anglican Pacifist Fellowship which renounces modern war and the preparation to wage modern war. I think of myself as a 'Christian and a pacifist', rather than a 'Christian pacifist' which would overstate the contribution that faith makes. I believe pacifism is the correct and rational response to war in the twenty-first century, and that Jesus' call to love others including our enemies – a teaching with parallels in other great wisdom traditions – underlines this. This concept of non-aggression is reinforced by Jesus' vulnerability and crucifixion, such that God is not identified with our fears or the punitive urge towards violent retaliation if we are attacked, but with the victim. In the context of nuclear deterrence and the preparation to wage nuclear war, the teachings and example of Jesus should surely seek to lead us beyond fear and the threat of extermination as a basis for international relations.

*The Church and the Bomb* makes the point in a similar way:

> Human dignity and freedom are most certainly foundation values both for the Christian and the humanist. But it is precisely the glory of humankind that can be defended by means other than simple force of arms. These other means, whether seen in the cross of Jesus or in the witness of martyrs belonging to Christian or other faiths, in the corporate non-violence of Gandhi or in the enduring courage of dissidents in Eastern Europe and the Soviet Union, face them with a long and agonising path to tread.[17]

The dualistic rationale of faith and reason tends towards a liberal pacifism. With less dependence on a particular theological view, it is easier to accept that non-pacifist interpretations of scripture and tradition may be equally valid. This fosters humility in the way religious pacifism is presented, acknowledging that it is not necessarily 'without error'. Martin Luther King, who developed a 'realistic' doctrine when he came to understand that pacifism is not sinless but the lesser evil, made such a point in his autobiography: 'Many pacifists', he said, 'failed to see this: all too many had an unwarranted optimism concerning man and leaned unconsciously toward self-righteousness.'[18] When the nature and limitations of faith are forgotten, such positions can sometimes be blind to new demands brought about by changing circumstances. The refrain from *Anthem* is relevant here: it holds a message for anyone who takes an absolutist position when it says: 'Forget your perfect offering, there is a crack in everything, that's how the light gets in.'

Perhaps Mohandas Gandhi understood this when he explained his decision to accept the Indian Congress' decision to fight alongside the allies in the Second World War by saying: 'My aim is not to be consistent with my previous statements on a given question, but to be consistent with truth as it may present itself at a given moment.'[19] When we reflect on how revolutionary ideas like pacifism are implemented and become evolutionary realities, the crucial test is whether, at the core, the idea makes sense for the future. The intellectual context into which the question of nuclear abolition is placed should reflect this to avoid the common trap of judging the prospects for future eventualities by past and present circumstances.

But in the final analysis, implementation is about the attitude to risk, and in the words of *Anthem*: 'not dwelling on what has passed away or what is yet to be'.

## Security and deterrence

Arguments against pacifism revolve around the fact that disarmament makes us and those close to us more vulnerable. Certainly we have responsibilities here, but the Christian is taught to trust in God and take risks, especially for a just cause, whatever this may be. At the collective level, individual choice is constrained by the degree of security that the nation wants, as seen by its defence spending and military alliances formed (although, of course, one might still be a conscientious objector or a military tax refuser). But history tells us that military expenditure often depends more on political ideology and the desire for power than a need for security *per se*.

The development of nuclear weapons puts a completely different scope on these concerns. The crux is that nuclear weapons have the power to destroy the enemy's cities, and if necessary to annihilate his whole society. Whatever we think of the wisdom of such a strategy, the wickedness to which it consents cannot be denied. It envisages committing exactly the crime against 'God and Man' which the Second Vatican Council, with nuclear weapons very much in mind, had condemned unequivocally in 1965 (*Gaudium et Spes*, p. 80). It is simply morally wrong for any mortal to be invested with the authority to call into question the survival of the planet.

The pacifist position is clear and consistent. Nuclear weapons should not have been developed. Those that exist should be dismantled on a unilateral basis if necessary, and we should all be working towards a nuclear-free world (as part of the general abolition of war as a method of settling international disputes). But in these late times, can the world realistically go for zero nuclear weapons? I believe so, but it is important to be realistic about the dangers, particularly since future world politics are unlikely to be as mature and generous as some of the abolitionists imply. Humanity will be trying to survive the converging catastrophes of the twenty-first century, what James Howard Kunstler in his recent book calls *The Long Emergency*;[20] and there is bound to be some nuclear breakout as national leaders abuse their power and terrorists gain access to these weapons. 'The wars they will be fought again, the holy dove be bought again' in the words from *Anthem*. But, hopefully these risks will be nothing compared with risks of going on for ever and ever with nuclear weapons in national arsenals. (Strategies for minimizing the risk associated with nuclear disarmament were discussed in detail in Rotblat, Steinberger, and Udgaonkar.)[21]

## What of the future: threats and realities

Abolition will require major sacrifices by the more powerful nations, but these could occur in the development of a morality grounded in self-interest. As the world globalizes and becomes integrated, it makes more sense to worry about people far away who may impact dangerously on our lives. We might quibble about the term 'morality' when the logic is essentially self-interest; but the pursuance of that logic requires an act of true moral imagination akin to the words of Jesus. If we are going to find a way to make disadvantaged nations and their people happier and less resentful, we have to imagine ourselves in their shoes. We should seek to remove the reasons for conflict by working for justice and peace and steadily reduce national dependence on military forces. To achieve this as a global ethos would be a momentous accomplishment.

Realism says that abolition should be phased because of future uncertainties. And at the risk of appearing inconsistent, I would argue for a final step of holding limited nuclear weapons in the hands of a responsible international agency until the world is as safe as it can reasonably be.

Other existing weapons of mass destruction could to a large extent be swept up with the abolition of nuclear weapons. But a question mark would remain over new scientific discoveries which, in the wrong hands, could lead to a devastating next generation of military weapons (as the earlier quote from Jo Rotblat implies). Should we expect governments to regulate science in order to discourage harmful developments? Indeed, should the basic research that led to nuclear weapons ever have been carried out?

The problem here is that scientific research is inherently inefficient and unpredictable, and the only way in which humankind can secure all the advantages of knowledge is to enquire in every possible direction. Nowhere is freedom more important that where our ignorance is greatest – at the boundaries of knowledge, in other words where nobody can predict what lies ahead. Timothy Ferris[22] discusses the issues well and points out that the case for freedom snaps into focus when we look back into history. He asks rhetorically: 'Does this mean that the Swiss government ought to have prevented Einstein from publishing his special relativity paper in 1905, or that the UK Parliament ought to have padlocked Rutherford's laboratory before he could infer the structure of the atomic nucleus?' and follow with the point that: 'Government restrictions on scientific research seldom if ever make sense, except of course to enforce existing laws against broader abuses, such as fraud and assault, because they assume a 20/20 foresight that neither government nor anyone else possesses.'

One could in this context envisage a responsibility on the international agency referred to above to maintain a watching brief on emerging scientific knowledge to ensure that the potentials for abuse are understood and appropriate measures taken.

## Speaking truth to power

Now let me return again to militarism which is my main point.

A powerful military–industrial complex with strong political lobbying power, as it exists in the US and some other nations, is extremely dangerous for two reasons. First, it has a vested interest in promoting militarism and arms sales, if not actual military conflict; and arms negotiations, hidden as they often are from public scrutiny, are easily influenced by bribery and corruption.[23] This means that governments can be induced to buy weapons and view the military force as the ultimate option, such that in a situation of international tension, other non-violent options are not properly explored and military intervention promoted. And second, related to militarism *per se*, there is the danger that a strong military capability may fall into the hands of unscrupulous leaders who are bent on using it whatever happens.

The Church has a responsibility to speak truth to power, to weaken and eventually eliminate these dangers. When a situation is black and white and much is at stake, it is not enough to say, as in *Peacemaking in a Nuclear Age*, that its role is simply to deepen and broaden the discussion. Evil is evil and should be named. The run-up to the recent Iraq War is a case in point. It is clear now that the intelligence and the 'facts' were fixed by the Bush administration around its chosen policy, which was to attack Iraq. Clearly a country like the US with a large military capability only requires a group of ideological and self-possessed leaders in power, and an uncritical media, to wage an unjust war of global significance. The existence of a compliant ally under 'a special relationship' also helps.

The value of the just-war doctrine is bound to depend critically on its capability to resist such a dangers. The discourse is complicated, involving serious theology, legal considerations and much insider knowledge. Consequently, the churches have a responsibility to explain to Christians, in simple terms, what is actually going on. The key issue is to say clearly whether a military build-up or involvement in a conflict can be brought within the scope of the authority on which governments may normally call and be undertaken in such a manner as to establish justice.

The responsibility of individual Christians also needs to be emphasized. Oliver O'Donovan summarizes this well when he points out that all Christians are responsible before God in relation to other members of society who, of course, have their own differently responsible positions. The decisions are ours and cannot be thrown off because we have elected representatives (which he calls 'politically responsible deciders'), among whom we have to deliberate sympathetically and collaboratively. He says: 'God's peace is a practical demand laid on us. We must deny any "right" to the pursuit of any claim on the part of a people that it may sacrifice its neighbours in the cause of its own survival or prosperity.'[24]

This all implies the need for a worldwide civil movement that will set the agenda to wind down world militarism and move leaders to act.

The most difficult task is how Christians speak truth to power at the most difficult time when politically motivated decisions about militarism are being made or actual military action imminent. Here the words of Ched Myers are very relevant. He emphasized that Christianity should be grounded in the real world and in the life and passion of Jesus. We are obliged to monitor the way militarism and wars develop in future because we (and the churches) keep getting caught by surprise. He says:

> If we wait for the drums of war without figuring out how the last war affected us, we will just roll over. This is because war time is the worst time for Christians to determine their position of war. So much so that the politicians can soften us up by the propaganda give timelines for the ending of hostilities and grand visions . . . War surprises us.[25]

In this regard, the long period of talking about, working up to and positioning around the recent war against Iraq could have been used by the churches to school their members and all people of good will in the relevance of the just-war doctrine; and to rehearse them in approaching decisions that may need to be made soon as they face their Christian responsibilities. Such an approach is important because a deliberating public would elicit a more conscientious performance from its representatives, political and military.

Now, more than ever before, the churches as key opinion-forming bodies should be encouraging political action against militarism. There can be no room for confusion over what 'pre-emption' means. There is no justification for Britain to introduce a new generation of nuclear weapons; it should be decommissioning its existing capability.

## Humankind should fulfil its destiny

Although the Bible begins with a world in which God is actively and visibly involved with humanity, it does not end that way; and history continues the trend. God gradually disappears and speaks less and less, moving from the personal father in heaven to a more distant phenomenon out there somewhere, or for some, inwards to the ground of our being.

The twentieth century's rise of science and technology has not only contributed to the feeling of the disappearance of God; it has contributed to the feeling of a shift in the divine–human balance of control more than anything or any time in our history. For better or worse, technology, with its *bête noire* of nuclear weapons, has enormously strengthened humanity's grip on its destiny. It is pushing society to a point that demands a moral transformation fostering friendship and trust between nations.

As Richard Friedman has remarked, it may be that humanity 'needs a period of divine hiddenness, out of the manifest presence of God, to grow up and become all that we can be'.[26] The metaphor of parent and children suggests a coming of age when we shall be able to meet God on more equal terms, an idea central to the Kabbalah which also includes the notion that humans must endeavour to arrive at such a point.

Process theology develops these concepts. Here God is always with us in the evolution of his creation while at the same time beckoning all things towards a transcendent future. As we share this journey we begin to see the real nature of God as it becomes conscious of itself in humanity. But who says the journey has to be straightforward? The Kabbalist Isaac Luria, whose words inspired *Anthem*, told an entirely different creation story, full of false starts, divine mistakes, explosions, violent reversals and disasters.[27]

Humanity is in an inchoate period. Not surprisingly we are at a tipping point in environmental destruction and mass extinction in the natural world and a postmodernism characterized by a discontent at our decadent culture and bruising capitalism. Many seek the certainty of fundamentalist religions while new secular 'religions' are emerging. Perhaps a new redemptive myth will emerge which accepts that what has gone before was fundamentally in error, or at least misguided. This would herald a commitment to spirituality based on the wisdom traditions of Jesus and Buddha and the Golden Rule of treating others as you want them to treat you: a future time where there is no room for militarism.

Then, in the words of Leonard Cohen's *Anthem*, 'Every heart to love will come, but like a refugee.'

# 11 What are We Defending, Against Whom, with Nuclear Weapons?

## PETER JARMAN

The UK government has a responsibility to defend the lives, territory, homes and resources of energy and food of its citizens: our fundamental interests. In these post-Cold War years, which power or body might intend and be able to deprive us of this livelihood, and would the retention or modernizing of our Trident nuclear shield protect us? I feel strongly that the UK government should not plan to replace Trident and that it should implement steps under international supervision to place its existing nuclear warheads and their fissile material beyond use. In practice this would mean removing the warheads from the missiles, extracting their fissile material and diluting it or burning it in a nuclear reactor.

The UK currently has about 180 nuclear warheads of yield between 0.3 and 100 kilotonnes that can be fitted to American D5 missiles on its four Trident submarines. The yield of the Hiroshima uranium bomb was about 13 kilotonnes and that of the Nagasaki plutonium bomb about 6 kilotonnes of TNT equivalent. About a quarter of a million Japanese died from the effects of these bombs: half outright and half from their lingering aftermath, especially of radioactivity. A further quarter of a million are *hibakus*, surviving Japanese but suffering from effects of the bombs. However, had American forces needed to invade the Japanese mainland against the kind of fierce resistance displayed by Japanese forces on Okinawa, an estimated

40,000 to half a million Americans would have died and many more Japanese. Such moral and pragmatic dilemmas bedevil the underlying issues of the development, deployment and actual or possible use of nuclear weapons.

Nuclear weapons are indiscriminate weapons of mass destruction of people and the Earth's biosphere on which we live and move and have our being. Humankind has been very lucky to survive the nuclear weapons' confrontation of the Cold War years that was driven to the brink of annihilating most of the biosphere during the Cuban missile crisis.

As a person trained in pure and applied nuclear physics, I am appalled at the consequences of the innocent discovery of nuclear fission by Otto Hahn and Fritz Strassmann in Berlin in 1938 soon after their co-worker Lise Meitner, an Austrian Jew, fled to Stockholm. Investigating the effects of neutron-induced transmutations of uranium, rather than finding heavy elements like uranium, they discovered in the residue of the reactions an element that behaved like barium of half the atomic weight of uranium. It was barium: they had split the atom. (The uranium nucleus had split into rubidium and caesium nuclei, but the caesium isotope has a very short lifetime and decays into a barium isotope.) Their discovery was communicated to Meitner who contributed to the droplet model of the nucleus that revealed the immense amount of energy let loose in fission as the binding energy of a nucleus of half the atomic number of uranium is considerably more than that of uranium. Nuclear scientists also found out that for every incident neutron splitting a uranium nucleus, several neutrons were released. They realized that a chain reaction was possible yielding a catastrophic amount of energy if uncontrolled as in a bomb, but yielding a useful source of energy in a nuclear reactor if carefully controlled through moderators and control rods.

A fairly simple calculation that undergraduate physicists can do will determine the minimum or critical size of fissile material for such a chain reaction: it is about 50 kg for a bare sphere of uranium 235 which can be reduced to about 15 kg if a neutron reflector is placed around the sphere. The Hiroshima bomb contained 60 kg of uranium 235. The critical masses of plutonium 239 are smaller, about 10 kg for a bare sphere. The Nagasaki bomb contained 6.4 kg of sub-critical plutonium 239 that was compressed by an imploding spherical shockwave generated by TNT to increase its density above the chain reaction threshold.

Plutonium does not exist naturally and is made atom by atom in nuclear reactors through the action of neutrons on the non-fissile uranium 238. Natural uranium contains only 0.7 per cent of uranium 235: weapons grade uranium has to be made by a laborious means of gaseous diffusion or centrifugal separation – it is much easier and less expensive to produce plutonium in a reactor whether for military or peaceful purposes. Several hundred tonnes of this man-made element now exist and can readily be transported. The UK is believed to have about eight tonnes of plutonium 239 and about 22 tonnes of enriched uranium in stock.

Far more energy on an atom-to-atom basis can be released by the fusion of hydrogen into helium, a process that fuels the sun: at its centre, at a temperature of several million degrees, four million tonnes of hydrogen a second are burnt to give an incident radiation flux at the top of the Earth's atmosphere of about 1400 watts per square meter, neither too much nor too little to sustain the biosphere, including humankind. The energy per quantum of visible radiation is about one electron volt which drives photosynthesis and causes no harm to humans, unlike radiation of about one million electron volts per quantum of nuclear energy which causes massive radiation damage leading to a lingering death over many years.

This considerable increase in energy from fusion rather than from fission arises because the binding energy of a lithium nucleus is greater than that of hydrogen or deuterium, heavy hydrogen, by a larger factor than the binding energy of the nuclear fragments of uranium compared to the uranium nucleus. The development of fusion bombs in the 1950s by the USSR, USA, the UK and France had yields of up to 300 megatonnes of TNT equivalent compared to a maximum of about 50 kilotonnes with a fission bomb. The fusion substance was generally lithium deuteride, which was ignited by radiative implosion from a fission device. To increase the blast and radiation fall-out a shell of uranium 238 was placed around the bomb that under the conditions generated by the fusion would itself exceed its fission threshold: a fission–fusion–fission bomb resulted. The development of these super-bombs served no military purposes, since for example ten or twelve of them would completely annihilate the UK. As I shall describe, they were developed to satisfy political and psychological drives, including the personality traits of key scientists and politicians.

I was struck by these personality characteristics when I shared the same boat as Otto Hahn and Werner Heisenberg in 1957 on an excursion from Lindau to the island of Mainau on Lake Constance during a gathering of Nobel prizewinners for physics that I attended as a postgraduate. I discerned that Hahn was more of an introverted personality and I believed him when he said that nuclear energy should not be used for weapons, whereas Heisenberg seemed to me to be more of an extrovert who could have let himself be a tool of Nazi power in advocating the development of nuclear weapons by Hitler during the war. Thank goodness that the Nazis were not prepared to allocate the huge resources needed for this, although Heisenberg and his team were well on their way to developing a nuclear reactor until British SAS agents destroyed the heavy water on its way from Norway to provide a moderator for it. Edward Teller, the 'father of the hydrogen bomb', seems to me to have had a troublesome personality, possibly arising as a Hungarian refugee with a pathological hatred of communism that drove him to promote the development of the hydrogen bomb at his Livermore laboratory in California during the 1950s, for which he persuaded Congress to invest huge funding.

In its duty to provide defence and security to its citizens, the UK government has a duty to be clear about what is being defended, against whom, and with what? Strategic defence reviews address these issues. There are threats to this security that are currently quite different from those experienced or feared during the Cold War years, primarily the threats of terrorist activity and from rogue states. During the Cold War years, nuclear weapons were seen to be the ultimate deterrent if all else failed against Soviet expansionism. In the UK their possession was seen to be an alternative to the conscription of civilians for military purposes. The exercise of Mutually Assured Destruction required our nuclear weapons to be ready to fire within minutes, and for them to be primed and targeted so that they could even be fired merely on a warning of an impending nuclear strike against the UK. Indeed, the warning might have been so short that computers took over most of the decision-making about when and if to use our nuclear weapons. At least the UK's Trident nuclear missiles are currently on standby and would take days to be targeted and ready to fire.

The US is seeking to develop small-yield nuclear weapons, mini-nukes, that could be very accurately targeted to penetrate underground stores of biological and chemical weapons. While there seems to be no problem in principle in reducing the yield of nuclear weapons, there is a limit to which any bomb can penetrate the Earth, and stores of weapons could be built well below this depth. Nuclear devices exploded underground have far more blast effect than those detonated above ground, while having similar radioactive fall-out. The high temperature realized close to the explosion would neutralize some of these weapon arsenals but in the blast much would be released that would be hazardous to life. As argued by Hugh Beach in this book, conventional armed attacks would be far more effective and far less hazardous than the use of mini-nukes against these targets. There is also a danger that the testing of sophisticated mini-nukes would require an abrogation of the decision of the

US Congress to proscribe nuclear weapon testing and that such a regressive move would trigger off a resumption of nuclear weapons' tests by other powers.

Nuclear weapons or other weapons of mass destruction are of no use against a small militant group. However, against rogue states such as Saddam's Iraq it might be argued that nuclear weapons are a necessary deterrent. Israel apparently holds that view against threats of annihilation by neighbouring states.

Against such a view I suggest that the possession of nuclear weapons by any state encourages others to possess them too: Iran wants to have them because Israel does; Pakistan has them because India has them. To my mind these weapons serve only to alienate states from one another rather than finding some means of accommodation between them. By accommodation I mean that while not resolving the fundamental conflicts and contradictions between states, states can be encouraged to find ways of existing side by side without threatening each other with any weapons of mass destruction, of which biological weapons are a more major hazard than nuclear weapons for they can more easily be hidden and transported. Naturally injustice has to be addressed, such as the squeezing of Palestinians off their own territory by Israeli settlements and their security requirements.

Setting aside the need to possess nuclear weapons in order to sit at the top table with other nuclear states, there remains the query of whether the UK should deploy nuclear weapons as a protection against rogue states. By rogue states I understand those nations with little or no democratic control over their leadership that threaten to attack or eliminate another nation, or to seize or control strategic resources essential to the UK's well-being. Saddam's Iraq was one such case threatening neighbouring states including Israel, and suspected of having weapons of mass destruction – indeed having used chemical weapons against its own Kurdish population. Threatening such a state with nuclear attack, quite apart from the morality of such a use of weapons of mass destruction, is likely to have little remedial effect, for in a terminal crisis the Saddams and Hitlers of this world are indifferent to the sufferings of their own people.

There have to be alternative strategies for coping with rogue states. Invading them with superior force as in the case of Iraq has proved so far to be counter-productive. Saddam was barely touched by the sanctions imposed by the UN Security Council that killed hundreds of thousands of Iraqis. Rather than alienating such a regime, means need to be found to open it out by increasing the communication of its citizens at all levels with the rest of the world, promoting a civil society within it and addressing any just cause of grievances that its peoples and government may have.

Nuclear weapons serve political rather than military purposes. I discern that there are pervasive psychological forces underlying the past and present possession of nuclear weapons by governments, and that to eliminate them these psychological factors need to be laid bare and addressed. They may be considered in Buddhist terms to belong to the poisons of self-delusion that if nurtured can lead to great suffering.

Can the issues of group psychology be distinguished from those of political or defence strategy? The Manhattan project at Los Alamos to develop a nuclear weapon was largely driven by the fear that Nazi Germany might get there first. The rivalry between the United States and the Soviet Union over the development of the 'super', a hydrogen bomb, was driven by the anxiety that if they have it, we must. The case for Britain developing nuclear weapons was even more bizarre: Ernest Bevin in the autumn of 1946 over-rode the hesitations of Hugh Dalton and Stafford Cripps in exclaiming: 'We've got to have it. I don't want any other Foreign Secretary to be talked at or by the United States Secretary of State as I have just been. We've got to have this thing over here, whatever it costs. We've got to have the bloody Union Jack on top of it.' 'We need it, and the hydrogen bomb later, to reserve a place at the high table', said several British Prime Ministers: 'to secure our place above the salt at the negotiating table', remarked Sir Alec Douglas-Home. 'We must do it,' said Churchill, 'it's the price we pay to sit at the top table': 'so that we can discuss on equal terms with the United States and the Soviet Union', added Harold Macmillan. 'We cannot go naked into the conference chamber', remarked Aneurin Bevan in 1957.

Surely we have grown out of these delusions? The current problems of updating the composition of the UN Security Council, a top table, is not dependent on which nation has nuclear weapons and which does not. The fact that there are no Muslim nations among its five permanent members is felt by Muslims to be humiliating, and yet this is not affected by the fact that of Muslim nations only Pakistan has them.

Did the possession of nuclear weapons by both superpowers during the Cold War years keep the peace between them? This proposition is hard to sustain since we do not know if aggression would have occurred if they did not possess them. A similar reservation could be made about the preservation of peace between India and Pakistan as they both possess nuclear weapons. Nuclear weapons systems have a dreadful logic about them: 'The bigger and more powerful weapons that we can develop, the better' said Edward Teller in promoting a second nuclear weapons development facility at his Livermore laboratories. At the height of the Cold War, each superpower possessed tens of thousands of these weapons that could be launched even on warning of an imminent nuclear attack. It was as close to the Gadarene swine driven to death by being possessed of evil spirits that humankind has ever got to.

The many strategic arms reduction negotiations that focused on numbers of various weapons systems obscured fundamental discussions about what they were for and in what circumstances they would be used. The Soviet government and its think-tanks asserted that they had neither the intention nor the capability of invading the West, and yet the West remained apprehensive. A large array of theatre (tactical) nuclear weapons as well as medium- and long-range nuclear-tipped strategic missiles was arrayed against them, to which the Soviet Union responded in a tit-for-tat fashion. The Western response was also triggered by the concern over the superiority of the Soviets' conventional forces, especially of manpower. It seems to me that each side's nuclear posturing was continually based on taking the worse case analysis of their adversary rather than on establishing intentions and capabilities.

'It was necessary', said Clement Attlee, 'that our own nuclear weapons should be independent of the United States, whose interests might not always coincide with ours.' This case for independence from the United States has now fallen flat on its face as Britain's Trident warheads are now placed on American missiles, and the prior permission of the US government would surely be needed before the UK used them, since the enemy would not know which country had fired the missile and would presumably retaliate on both.

There would seem to be some deluded sense of virility about possessing nuclear weapons, a kind of phallic symbol. Predominantly a male delusion, I wonder? Is there also an element of moral superiority about this: we are the country that can be trusted with them, unlike rogue nations?

There is another element of nuclear posturing that seems to have a daredevil aspect about it. We will keep any potential enemy continually guessing about what our response will be to their perceived aggression. So long as we possess nuclear weapons, the greater will be the enemy's apprehension about confronting us. We actually do not intend to use them at all, under any circumstances, but having them will increase that apprehension and will deter aggression. But naturally we must be prepared to use them, otherwise they are not a true and honest deterrent. Brian Wicker exposes the moral bankruptcy of such a policy elsewhere in this book.

Could we consider the retention and updating of Britain's Trident nuclear weapons to be a shrewd insurance against some adversarial state that might emerge in several decades' time? The premium will be high: maybe £20 to £50 billion to update Trident? What needs to be sacrificed in alternative defence provision or other major government responsibilities to its citizens to release so large a sum? That is not the only cost: any further testing of more sophisticated warheads would be contrary to the provisions of the comprehensive test ban treaty; their retention, let alone increase in yield, would be contrary to the Nuclear Non-Proliferation Treaty. Does our preoccupation about whether to update our Trident weapons deter us from giving priority to what really threatens our security, such as climate change and population pressures?

Enough of this nuclear madness: we are not Gadarene swine about to drown. We can heed the need to be exorcized of our Trident weapons and any nuclear illusions of grandeur.

# 12 Is There a Military Rationale for the UK Retaining Its Nuclear Weapons?

## HUGH BEACH

Tim Hare, the former Director for Nuclear Policy in the British Ministry of Defence, has commented as follows on UK nuclear policy as set out in the 1998 Strategic Defence Review.[1]

> The policy makes it clear that the role of nuclear weapons is fundamentally political and that therefore any rationale for their retention is political. The UK does not possess nuclear weapons as part of the military inventory, they have no function as war-fighting weapons or to achieve lesser military objectives . . . They are indeed 'special' and reason enough not to put them into the hands of generals and admirals for the achievement of military goals.

Coming from such a well-informed source, this statement seems to dispose finally of the question posed in the title of this paper. But not everyone takes so dismissive a view. In July 2005 a Chinese General spoke publicly and matter-of-factly about the likelihood that if the United States interfered in a clash between China and Taiwan, nuclear weapons would be used.[2] More to the point, if Hare is right, why are NATO's doctrine and deployment still based on a quite different hypothesis: why are the Americans apparently moving back towards a policy of the greater usability of nuclear weapons to fulfil military objectives?

## NATO nuclear doctrine and forward basing

The classical NATO nuclear policy emerged in a series of 'guidelines' put out between 1967 and 1972.[3] The aim was to defend at three levels: direct defence (which meant conventional defence) against a non-nuclear attack for as long as possible; controlled escalation through the use of tactical nuclear weapons (TNW); and finally general nuclear response if all else failed. These guidelines, under the general rubric of 'flexible response', involved the overt acceptance of 'first use' by NATO as a last resort. This policy was given substance by the development of weapons systems to match. Air forces were equipped with free-falling and guided bombs and air-to-surface guided missiles. Navies, in addition to aircraft bombs, developed nuclear depth-charges and anti-submarine rockets. Armies were equipped with nuclear artillery of various calibres and free-flight rockets. Ground-launched cruise missiles, land mines and surface-to-air defence missiles were all given nuclear warheads. This force posture was developed at a time when Soviet conventional forces in Western Europe were held to outnumber NATO's by a factor of three to one or more.[4] The dismemberment of the Warsaw Pact and of the Soviet Union, followed by the expansion of NATO, has meant that the ratio of conventional forces as between Russia and NATO has been more than reversed. Most of NATO's TNW systems have been mothballed or destroyed. It might have been expected that these facts would lead to some reconsideration of the doctrine. But no such change has taken place. Thus Mr Hoon, British Secretary of State for Defence, in a written answer to a parliamentary question on 11 July 2002, said:

> A policy of no first use of nuclear weapons would be incompatible with our and NATO's doctrine of deterrence, nor would it further nuclear disarmament objectives. We have made clear, as have our NATO allies, that the circumstances

in which any use of nuclear weapons might have to be contemplated are extremely remote. Our overall strategy is to ensure uncertainty in the mind of any aggressor about the exact nature of our response, and thus to maintain effective deterrence.[5]

This makes it clear that NATO's policy still remains one of flexible response, involving the possibility of first use of nuclear weapons as a last resort.

Even more surprising is that, as a counterpart to this doctrine, American TNW are still held ready for use on the territory of six non-nuclear members of NATO and in the UK. These arrangements date from the late 1950s and early 1960s when bi-lateral Programmes of Co-operation were concluded between these countries and the US, most of which remain in force today. The weapons are stored in specially constructed vaults on 12 airfields: three each in Germany and Turkey, two in Italy, and one each in Belgium, the Netherlands, Greece and the UK. The weapons are B-61 gravity bombs, delivered by strike aircraft. All the aircraft are dual capable, being specially equipped for nuclear munitions in addition to their normal role. The crews are trained and exercised in peacetime for their possible nuclear missions. The nuclear weapons are all owned by the US and in peacetime they remain under the sole control of the US Air Force. In most cases (but not the UK) they would be transferred to the partner nations in the event of war. The vaults have a total capacity of 360 weapons but it is believed that the holding of live weapons is about half this, say 150–180 bombs. The vaults were being refurbished in 2005 to keep them operational until 2018. The costs to the US Air Force of providing and storing the weapons and to the Allied Air Forces of owning and operating the aircraft are said to be 'extraordinarily high'.[6]

Common sense would suggest that both the policy and practice of 'nuclear sharing' are out of date and should be scrapped. Why has this not happened? It seems clear that the continued presence of American TNW in Europe is due more to institutional paralysis than to logic: the desire to demonstrate America's continued commitment to European security, some vague concept of risk and burden sharing among NATO Allies, or, most absurdly, adherence to the simplistic concept 'No nukes, no troops'. As Mr Hoon said, in a written answer to the House of Commons on 1 February 2002: 'Some US nuclear weapons remain based in the UK in accordance with long-standing NATO policy. Nuclear forces based in Europe and committed to NATO provide an essential political and military link between the European and North American members of the Alliance.'[7] It would be more rational to argue that Europe and the US share a common interest in reducing the thousands of Russian tactical nuclear warheads in Europe left over from the Cold War. As long ago as 1997, in Helsinki, Russia and the US mooted further measures to reduce tactical nuclear systems, but nothing has come of them. If the six non-nuclear members of NATO who currently train for a tactical nuclear role were ready to give this up, it could open the way for repatriating all the remaining American TNW. This would meet Russia's long-standing wish to rid European territory of nuclear weapons within range of her territory. It could act as an important confidence-building measure and encourage further reductions on the Russian side. In view of America's acute reluctance to enter into fresh treaty commitments, an exchange of unilateral announcements might be the best method. Meanwhile increased transparency in this area is a necessary first step.

## The US nuclear policy

Great concern has been aroused by the American Nuclear Posture Review submitted to Congress on 31 December 2001, of which excerpts have become publicly available.[8] It establishes a New Triad consisting of:

- Offensive strike systems, both nuclear and non-nuclear.
- Defences, both active and passive.
- A revitalized defence infrastructure.

These are bound together with enhanced command, control and information systems. In his covering letter to Congress, Secretary of Defence Donald Rumsfield said that the result would be to make the US less dependent than it has been in the past on nuclear forces to provide its offensive deterrent capability. But several of the proposals in the report suggested, on the contrary, a greater emphasis on nuclear weapons.

1  The report gave examples of 'immediate contingencies' for which the US must be prepared in setting requirements for nuclear strikes. These included a North Korean attack on South Korea or a military confrontation over the status of Taiwan. It listed also Iran, Syria and Libya among countries that could be involved in such contingencies, on the grounds that all sponsored or harboured terrorists and all had active programmes to develop weapons of mass destruction and missiles.
2  Under the heading of an 'Advanced Concepts Initiative', proposals were made for modifying existing nuclear weapons to provide additional yield flexibility, improved earth-penetrating weapons and reduction of collateral damage.

Taken together, these clearly implied a renewed willingness to regard nuclear weapons as useful and indeed usable weapons.

Even more alarmingly, a draft document, the Doctrine for Joint Nuclear Operations JP 3–12, appeared on the Pentagon website in the summer of 2005.[9] This related specifically to the use of nuclear weapons within a theatre, i.e., tactically. It said that such use required that nuclear and conventional plans must be co-ordinated to the greatest extent possible. And it gave examples of conditions under which theatre commanders could request Presidential authority to use nuclear weapons. These included:

- An adversary using or intending to use weapons of mass destruction against US or Allied forces or civilian populations.
- Imminent attack from adversary biological weapons that only nuclear weapons can safely destroy.
- Attacks on adversary installations including weapons of mass destruction, deep hardened bunkers containing chemical or biological munitions or the command infrastructure required to attack the US or its Allies.
- To counter potentially overwhelming adversary conventional forces including mobile and area targets (troop concentrations).
- For rapid and favourable war termination on US terms.
- To ensure success of US and multinational operations.
- To demonstrate US intent and capability to use nuclear weapons to deter adversary use of weapons of mass destruction.
- To respond to adversary-supplied weapons of mass destruction use by surrogates against US or allied forces or civilian populations.

The Pentagon has now formally withdrawn this document, but this is simply to remove it from the public domain and from the Pentagon's internal reading list.[10] The point, however, is that this document represents an explicit and internally coherent doctrine for the tactical use of nuclear weapons, which has found favour at a senior level. Those who regard this as a disastrous way of thinking have focused on two projects in particular: 'bunker-busting' and 'mini-nukes'.

### *'Bunker-busting'*

The case for developing a nuclear warhead specifically for the defeat of hardened and deeply buried targets (HDBTs) rests on the alleged existence of over 1,400 underground facilities, known or suspected, for use by potential enemies as command centres, refuges or stores for missiles and nuclear, biological or chemical weapons. We are told that the depth of these structures, together with their steel and concrete reinforcements, call for highly accurate intelligence and precise weapon delivery. They may defeat any attack by conventional weapons.[11] In 1997 the US added an earth-penetrating version of the B61 bomb to its nuclear arsenal. But tests have shown that it could penetrate only about 20 feet into dry earth when dropped from 40,000 feet. This means it could not destroy very deeply buried bunkers or caves. Nor is there any prospect that the radioactivity of the weapon's nuclear burst could be contained.[12] According to one well-founded calculation, a weapon twice the length of the B61, even if accelerated by a rocket, could not penetrate more than about 80 feet. The fallout produced by a one-kiloton warhead at that depth would kill everyone on the surface within a radius of about half a mile in still air. Wind could carry it for tens of miles.[13] The new warhead would apparently be designed 'with a much lower yield . . . producing less fallout by a factor of ten or twenty'.[14] But lethal fallout would still be bound to result.

In any case, the notion of 'bunker-busting' is beset with practical difficulties. How is one to determine the location of such bunkers with the necessary pinpoint accuracy – unless of course our own troops are already there, in which case better methods suggest themselves? What is to be done if the bunkers have been thoughtfully located under schools, hospitals or apartment blocks? How can one be sure which bunkers are occupied anyway? If the target to be attacked is believed to contain chemical, biological or nuclear weapons material, how can one be sure of incinerating it all, rather than distributing it in active form over a large area? It is therefore welcome news that funding for this project has been dropped from the Fiscal 2006 budget at the request of the National Nuclear Security Administration of the

Energy Department. It looks as though this project may now be dead since the statement added that the Defence Department will now focus its research into earth-penetrating technology using conventional weaponry.[15]

## 'Mini-nukes'

The case for 'mini-nukes' is less well defined. The Pentagon is said to be seeking a completely new warhead design with a yield of 5 kilotons or less. This could address one or more of the requirements set out in the NPR 'to attack mobile and re-locatable targets, to defeat chemical or biological agents, to improve accuracy and limit collateral damage'.[16] It is said that to rely on high-yield strategic weapons for such purposes would be self-deterring and the development of mini-nukes could ensure flexibility in decision-making. In particular, America has wanted to keep its opponents guessing as to how it would respond to chemical or biological attack. As an official explained in 1996: 'We think the ambiguity involved in the issue of nuclear weapons contributes to our own security, keeping any potential adversary who might use either chemical or biological [weapons] unsure of what our response might be.'[17] More recently, it seems that the veil of ambiguity has been to some extent set aside. According to a report in *The Washington Times* (31 January 2003) a classified document signed by President Bush on 14 September 2002 said: 'The United States will continue to make clear that it reserves the right to respond with overwhelming force – including potentially nuclear weapons – to the use of [weapons of mass destruction] against the United States, its forces abroad, and friends and allies.'

Congress has recently voted the sum of $25 million in the Financial Year 2006 for a different project known as the Reli-able Replacement Warhead (RRW).[18] The idea is to redesign new parts for America's ageing stockpile that would make the warheads more reliable, longer lived and safer to maintain. This makes perfect sense. But if there are to be new designs of warhead, might not these be built with new missions in mind – for example mini-nukes or even bunker-busters reintroduced by the back door?

## Is the increased usability of nuclear weapons for real?

During the heyday of tactical nuclear planning in NATO (during the 1950s and 1960s) target analysis for TNW concentrated on the blunting of dangerous enemy thrusts, the attack of troop concentrations (where the ability of neutron flux to penetrate armour and dug-in infantry positions with overhead cover was particularly useful), the destruction of bridges and the blocking of defiles – all but impossible by conventional weapons before the arrival of precision guidance – and the attack of dispersed relatively soft targets such as formation headquarters, anti-aircraft sites, supply dumps and communication nodes.[19] The draft doctrine quoted above seems to be harking back to the Cold War, as critics have been quick to point out.

The idea of using nuclear weapons against such targets today is highly implausible. This is not because the wars of today do not present such targets. The Taliban blocking approaches to Kabul, and the Iraqi Republican Guard defending Baghdad could certainly have been suitable for attack by F-15 or F-16 aircraft using B61 bombs; or by the mini-nukes said to be under consideration for attacking mobile and re-locatable targets, with improved accuracy and less collateral damage. But in every such case modern precision weapons coupled with carpet bombing by B-52s, tank-busting runs by A-10 and the use of C-130 gun-ships offer a far more cost-effective solution, 'minus the fallout'. And it need hardly be pointed out that the capture of a city that is being defended from house to house is as unsuitable a task for TNW as it is possible to imagine.

Still more implausible is the notion of using TNW in response to enemy use, or intending use, of chemical or biological weapons.

If the aim were to retaliate upon the source of these weapons one would either have to trace the missile launchers (a notoriously difficult task) or, in the case of bombs or crop-spray aircraft, to attack their bases, which are not a lucrative target for TNW. If, more plausibly, the aim is simply to punish the regime by 'making the strongest possible response', then of course anything goes. There is no call for accuracy or minimal fallout – why not a megaton strike on the seat of government or the power base of the ruler?

But simply to say this is to show why such a concept lacks all contact with reality. Frank von Hippel has pointed out that American presidents have in the past threatened to use nuclear weapons in situations which did not threaten the existence of the nation: Truman to force an armistice in Korea; Eisenhower to stop Chinese bombardment of islands in the Taiwan strait; Nixon to obtain a face-saving exit from the war in Vietnam. In the end they all realized that the political costs of breaking the nuclear taboo 'vastly outweighed the military benefits from nuclear weapon use'.[20] Today these political costs would be certain to include converting the whole of the Third World into violent revulsion against the US; greatly encouraging recruitment into anti-American terrorist organizations; destroying NATO; discrediting the United Nations beyond repair and fatally undermining the nuclear non-proliferation regime as more and more countries came to regard a nuclear insurance policy as indispensable in a world become radically more unpredictable. As many people have pointed out, 'Nukes are the only weapon that could pose a threat to US survival. Why would you want to open Pandora's box?[21]

## The UK

These arguments apply all the more strongly to the UK. The Ministry of Defence, in its *Report and Accounts, 2004–5*, says: 'The UK's nuclear weapons have a continuing use as a means of deterring major strategic military threats, and a continuing role in guaranteeing the ultimate security of the UK.'[22] The reference to 'major strategic military threats' carries a whiff of Cold War thinking, in line with the ossified NATO doctrine referred to above. No one can pretend to foresee with any precision the geo-political context of the mid-twenty-first century, but even as a worst case it is hard to envisage any power but Russia able to pose such a threat. Be that as it may, the 'use' and 'role' foreseen in this statement clearly refer to a deterrent at the political level rather than as a means of fighting a war. The British government has not, since the end of the Cold War, claimed any war-fighting role for its nuclear weapons. All battlefield or theatre nuclear weapons in British hands have been disposed of. The government has announced at the same time a 'substrategic' role for Trident in the following terms:

> The ability to undertake a massive nuclear strike is not enough to ensure deterrence. An aggressor might, in certain circumstances, gamble on a lack of will ultimately to resort to such a strike. We also need the capability to undertake nuclear action on a more limited scale in order to demonstrate our willingness to defend our vital interests to the utmost, and so to induce a political decision to halt aggression without inevitably triggering strategic nuclear exchanges.[23]

Malcolm Rifkind, then Defence Secretary, made it plain that this involved no concept of fighting and winning a war. It remained a question of deterrence, albeit at a slightly lower level than all-out retaliation.[24] As Richard Hatfield, then MOD Director of Policy explained, [the substrategic role] 'is a form of deterrence, not necessarily a specific weapon'.[25] According to Michael Quinlan, the essence of this strategy is to 'hold at risk a wide variety of military targets'. He explains as follows:

> It is this concept – the concept of a wide range of different options – that is now, and has been since the late 1960s, the

essence of NATO's defensive strategic concept. It is not a strategy of predetermined first nuclear use, nor of attempting somehow to fight or neutralise the opposing nuclear armoury, nor of massive nuclear use, nor of a rigidly fixed sequence of actions in progressive escalation. On the contrary it is precisely a strategy to provide political leaders with military choices of divers kinds so that they can respond on a carefully limited scale yet in a way relevant to whatever the circumstances may be, not using more force than necessary for the purpose of ending the conflict. It is important to recognize that, while the targets to be held at risk are military ones, the whole object is to transmit to any adversary a political message. In essence it is this: 'You have wholly underestimated my determination to defend my interests: for your own survival you must now stop.'[26]

This concept has much in common with the French notion of 'Pre-Strategic' use, as a shot across the bows of any intending aggressor or last-but-one resort. More recently President Chirac has expanded this concept to include use against 'the leaders of states who use terrorist methods against us'. He said that French nuclear warheads had already been 'reconfigured' to deal with the new threat and identified 'power centres' in hostile countries as potential targets. But he restated his opposition to the use of battlefield nuclear weapons and said he would not change France's policy of no 'first strike'.[27]

As regards British use of nuclear weapons in response to an enemy who used chemical or biological weapons, the British government has spoken with forked tongues. For example, in 2002 the then Defence Secretary Geoff Hoon said in a television interview, 'If there is a threat to our deployed forces, if they come under attack by weapons of mass destruction and by that specifically chemical, biological weapons, then we would reserve the option , in an appropriate case, . . . to use nuclear weapons'.[28] However, 18 months later Foreign Office Minister

Dennis MacShane told Parliament: 'The United Kingdom remains fully committed to the Negative Security Assurance we gave in 1995.'[29] On the face of it, this Assurance applies to any non-nuclear weapon state which possesses other weapons of mass destruction, i.e., biological and/or chemical weapons, even if those weapons were acquired in violation of commitments under the Biological and/or Chemical Weapons Conventions, and even if those weapons were used to attack the UK or UK forces.[30] But in any case, as explained above, a nuclear response to enemy use of chemical or biological weapons is most unlikely to take the form of battlefield use. It would represent a major escalation of the conflict and would be so clearly disproportionate and clearly illegal as to be barely credible. The apparently deliberate ambiguity on this point must contain a large element of bluff.

In replying to a Parliamentary Question, Defence Secretary John Reid has said that the 'Labour Party's manifesto for the 2005 general election made clear [its] commitment to retain the UK's independent nuclear deterrent. Although decisions on any replacement for Trident are likely to be taken in the current Parliament, it is too early to rule out, or rule in, any particular option.'[31] It is clear, therefore, so far as this government is concerned, that the question is not whether to replace Trident, but in what form. One such option is clearly to follow the Americans by stretching the operational life of the existing four Trident submarines[32] and replacing the existing D5 missiles by the upgraded version known as D5A. The life of these systems could apparently be extended to 2040. An alternative solution, possibly cheaper, might be to upgrade Tomahawk cruise missiles for long-range delivery and fit them with a new British-built nuclear warhead, to be launched from aircraft. The argument in this chapter has no bearing on the pros and cons of this issue save in one crucial respect. Buying a cruise missile version of the deterrent could be seen as lowering the nuclear threshold to the tactical level by giving the weapon a military function. As

Michael Meacher has pointed out – reflecting what are said to be widespread misgivings in the Parliamentary Labour Party: 'Frankly this is a neo-con idea for using tactical nuclear weapons rather than the massive Trident system.'[33] The question might then become not whether ministers wish to retain an independent British deterrent but whether they agree – or even half-agree – with the developing American doctrine of usable pre-emptive nukes.[34]

In the quotation at the beginning of this chapter Tim Hare asserted that 'the UK does not possess nuclear weapons as part of the military inventory, they have no function as war-fighting weapons or to achieve lesser military objectives'. It is greatly to be hoped that this statement continues to hold good.

*Note: This chapter was first published in 'The Future of Britain's Nuclear Weapons: Experts Debate the Issues', Current Decisions Report No. 28, Oxford Research Group, 28 March 2006. Debate 2.*

# 13  Non-Proliferation and Arms Control Aspects

## ROLAND SMITH

This chapter does not attempt to assess whether the replacement of the UK's existing nuclear capability at the time when new delivery systems are needed would be sensible, or a good use of resources, or morally justifiable. It is concerned with the narrower issue of the relevance to the decision of the UK's international non-proliferation and other arms control obligations. This question is not, of course, unrelated to the moral issue – there are probably no circumstances in which it can be morally justifiable for a state deliberately to ignore its freely undertaken international obligations – but it is nevertheless separate.

The most obvious issues to consider are those which arise from the Nuclear Non-Proliferation Treaty of 1968. It is frequently asserted that this Treaty constitutes a bargain between the non-nuclear weapon states and the nuclear weapon states whereby the former undertook not to acquire nuclear weapons in exchange for the latter undertaking to work for nuclear disarmament. In actual fact the Treaty is a good deal more complex than this, and none of its articles contains the simple proposition set out in the preceding sentence. There are good reasons for this. It can well be argued that it is the non-nuclear weapon states, or at least the vast majority of them, who have the strongest interest in preventing further nuclear proliferation, regardless of whether or not there is nuclear disarmament by the recognized nuclear weapon states, and therefore one of the important aspects of the Treaty is the bargain which it embodies between non-nuclear weapon states. Nonetheless, the Non-Proliferation Treaty does of course contain binding obligations on the nuclear weapon states – and the obligation concerning nuclear disarmament is that set out in Article VI, which reads 'Each of the Parties to the Treaty undertakes to pursue negotiations in good faith on measures relating to cessation of the nuclear arms race at an early date and to nuclear disarmament, and on a Treaty on general and complete disarmament under strict and effective international control.'

Like many articles in many international treaties, this Article is less than crystal clear in its wording, because it represents the outcome of a process of negotiation. But there are a number of striking features about the way in which it is phrased. First, although it is often referred to, without quoting its wording, as though it were an undertaking only by the nuclear weapon states, in fact it is an undertaking by all parties to the Treaty. This is clearly deliberate, because there is another Article of the Treaty – Article I – which is binding only on the nuclear weapon states, committing them not to transfer nuclear weapons or weapons technology to non-nuclear weapon states. Second, since it is about negotiations, it is not an undertaking which any one country can fulfil in isolation. Third, obviously some of what is required can only be delivered by certain parties. In particular, the phrase 'cessation of the nuclear arms race' obviously when it was written referred primarily if not exclusively to the activities of the United States and the Soviet Union; and indeed the whole SALT and START process, which originally began soon after the conclusion of the Non-Proliferation Treaty, can be seen in part as an attempt by those two countries, and subsequently by the United States and Russia, to fulfil their obligations under the Non-Proliferation Treaty. No one – except perhaps domestic critics of the British nuclear weapons programme, or people seeking to score a debating point with British interlocutors – has ever seriously accused the United Kingdom of engaging in a 'nuclear arms race'. With whom, after all, would the United Kingdom have been racing? Finally, the whole process of nuclear disarmament is itself set by the Article in the overall context of negotiations for a treaty on general and complete disarmament. The meaning, and indeed the credibility, of the concept of general and complete disarmament, is a subject for a book in itself. When I was dealing with arms control matters in the Foreign and Commonwealth Office, I used to think of it as a concept something like the Kingdom of Heaven, in that it provided a pole towards which one could strive to orientate oneself even while recognizing that one would never get there simply by one's own efforts. But at all events, the inclusion of the phrase in this Article is a clearly a recognition that there is an inter-relationship between nuclear disarmament and progress in other areas of arms control.

None of this is to suggest for a moment that the Article does not really commit the United Kingdom to anything. Moreover, in interpreting it, it is important to take account of subsequent international discussion. Many writers draw particular attention in this regard to the 1996 advisory opinion of the International Court of Justice on the legality of nuclear weapons. The Court stated that it could not reach a definitive conclusion as to the legality or illegality of the use of nuclear weapons by a state in an extreme circumstance of self-defence in which its very survival would be at stake. But it also said that:

> In the long run, international law, and with it the stability of the international order which it is intended to govern, are bound to suffer from the continuing difference of views with regard to the legal status of weapons as deadly as nuclear weapons. It is consequently important to put an end to this state of affairs: the long-promised complete nuclear disarmament appears to be the most appropriate means of achieving that result.

Taking into account the obligations set out in Article VI of the

Non-Proliferation Treaty, the Court concluded unanimously that: 'There exists an obligation to pursue in good faith and bring to a conclusion negotiations leading to nuclear disarmament in all its aspects under strict and effective international control.' It is important to note the official British government position that: 'The International Court of Justice opinion does not require a change in the United Kingdom's entirely defensive deterrence policy' (Baroness Symons, Hansard, House of Lords, 26 January 1998).

It is also of particular importance in considering the current significance of Article VI to take into account the various statements which have been made in the context of the Non-Proliferation Treaty review process. Ever since it came into force in 1970, the Treaty has, in accordance with Article VIII, been reviewed at five-yearly intervals, and the question of progress towards nuclear disarmament has always been one of the central themes for discussion. It is fair to say that at no time has the United Kingdom ever been singled out for special criticism during such discussions, even in the immediate aftermath of the decision to replace Polaris by Trident – bearing out Lawrence Freedman's prediction, in commenting on the relevance of Article VI in his book *Britain and Nuclear Weapons*, published in 1980, that:

There is no evidence that unilateral action by Britain, however . . . drastic, will have anything other than a marginal effect on the attitudes and behaviour of non-nuclear weapon states. A move to increase significantly Britain's nuclear capabilities, rather than simply maintain them at existing levels, would generate some criticism and would serve to underline the value that the nuclear weapon states continue to attach to their nuclear possessions. Nevertheless, a decision either way on the replacement of Polaris would make little difference to the success of the Non-Proliferation Treaty and other non-proliferation strategies.

Perhaps the relative absence of criticism from other parties to the Treaty, even though Trident represented a significant increase in capabilities over Polaris, stemmed from a recognition that the British government's choice of Trident was made not in order to achieve such an increase in capabilities but in order to preserve the advantages of commonality with the United States. Or perhaps it was simply that, even with the increase, the UK's capabilities were perceived as insignificant compared with those of the United States and the Soviet Union. But the fact that Britain did largely escape criticism from other parties to the Treaty at that time obviously does not absolve her of responsibility under Article VI now.

The most detailed ever elaboration of the collective understanding by parties to the Treaty of the requirements of Article VI was a document agreed at the Review Conference of 2000. This set out 13 steps towards nuclear disarmament, with the following introductory text: 'The Conference agrees on the following practical steps for the systematic and progressive efforts to implement Article VI of the Treaty on the Non-Proliferation of Nuclear Weapons.' Clearly, by joining in the consensus on the document as a whole, the UK accepted these commitments for itself. Moreover, several of the individual steps were based on proposals submitted by NATO or the European Union.

Of the 13 steps, two, one concerning START and the Anti-Ballistic Missile Treaty, and one concerning the Trilateral Initiative between the United States, Russia and the International Atomic Energy Agency, were clearly never of any relevance to the UK. Others, such as the negotiation in the CD[1] of a treaty banning the production of fissile material for nuclear weapons, while they involve the UK, are currently blocked for reasons which are outside the UK's control.

But others of the steps were clearly relevant to the UK. The first two were those regarding nuclear testing. The first step called for signatures and ratifications in order to achieve early entry into force of the Comprehensive Test Ban Treaty. The second called for a moratorium on nuclear weapon testing pending entry into force of the Treaty. The fifth step concerned the principle of irreversibility, and stipulated: 'the principle of irreversibility to apply to nuclear disarmament, nuclear and other related arms control and reduction measures'. Step 9 called *inter alia* for 'further efforts by the nuclear weapon states to reduce their nuclear arsenals unilaterally'; for 'the further reduction of non-strategic nuclear weapons, based on unilateral initiatives and as an integral part of the nuclear arms reduction and disarmament process'; for 'concrete and agreed measures to further reduce the operational status of nuclear weapons systems'; for 'further efforts by the nuclear weapon states to reduce their nuclear arsenals unilaterally'; for 'an unequivocal undertaking by the nuclear weapon states to accomplish the total elimination of their nuclear arsenals leading to nuclear dis-armament'; for 'steps by all the nuclear weapon states leading to nuclear disarmament in a way that promotes international stability, and based on the principle of undiminished security for all' and for 'a diminishing role for nuclear weapons in secu-rity policies to minimize the risk that these weapons might ever be used and to facilitate the process of their total elimination'.

It is, I think, an important principle that governments should not subscribe to statements of this kind unless they are seriously meant. The document in question was not in itself legally bind-ing, but the fact that it was agreed at a conference of the parties to an important international Treaty gives it considerable weight. It is correspondingly important that, having subscribed to the statement, the British and other governments concerned should not forget that they have done so. How, then, has the UK's actual performance matched up to these commitments? First of all, as regards the Comprehensive Test Ban Treaty, Britain has done everything possible. Together with France she was (on 6 April 1998) the first nuclear weapon state to ratify the Treaty, and she has not conducted a nuclear test since 1991. As

for the other commitments, it is clear that she has made significant reductions in her nuclear arsenal, and has been ready to
present these reductions as steps towards implementation of her
obligations under Article VI. On 3 May 2004, for example, at
the Preparatory Committee for the 2005 Non-Proliferation
Treaty Review Conference, British Ambassador David Broucher
said the following:

> Over the past twelve years the UK has made substantial
> progress on our global nuclear disarmament obligations under
> Article VI of the NPT. This has included the withdrawal and
> dismantling of our maritime tactical nuclear capability; the
> withdrawal and dismantling of the RAF's WE177 nuclear
> bomb; and the termination of the nuclear Lance missile and
> artillery roles that we undertook with US nuclear weapons
> held under the dual-key arrangements . . . We are the only
> Nuclear Weapon State to have reduced to a single system and
> on this point we are proud to be the most forward-leaning of
> the Nuclear Weapon States.

The UK cannot claim – and Ambassador Broucher did not
claim – to have eliminated non-strategic weapons, simply
because she has declared that Trident now has a sub-strategic as
well as a strategic role, even though acquired originally wholly
as a strategic system. However, the UK can claim to have
reduced the operational readiness of Trident, and the total
number of warheads. Ambassador Broucher went on to say:

> Our nuclear forces patrol on reduced readiness; only a single
> Trident submarine is now on deterrent patrol at any one
> time, normally at several days' 'notice to fire' and with its
> missiles de-targeted. We hold a total of less than 200 opera-
> tionally available warheads. This amounts to a total reduc-
> tion of 70% in the explosive power of our nuclear weapons
> since the end of the Cold War.

It seems to me that the claim that the UK has done a good deal to implement her Article VI commitments is a fair one. But would the acquisition of a successor to Trident be a reversal of this progress, and thus an indication that the UK had never really taken its commitments seriously? Clearly, there are those who would argue that it would indeed be a betrayal of all the UK's commitments to undertake any kind of modernization of its deterrent, at least unless that modernization also involved reductions. But I think this case is a difficult one to make, given that the UK already has the smallest arsenal of any of the nuclear weapon states. The UK sought in the Strategic Defence Review of 1998 to define and implement a concept of genuinely minimum deterrence – the Review stated that the reduced arsenal 'is the minimum necessary to provide for our security for the foreseeable future'. One can of course always dispute exactly what constitutes a minimum. But if the concept has any meaning, then the UK is obviously pretty close to it – it could not reduce the number of warheads much further without disarming completely. To argue that it does not have the right to take the steps necessary to maintain its deterrent at the existing level is in effect to demand of the nuclear weapon state least well placed to do so that it should take unilateral measures to compensate for the perceived failure of the larger nuclear weapon states, and in particular the United States and Russia, to do more to implement their own commitments.

It would be a very different matter if any proposal for the replacement of Trident were to involve an increase in the size of the UK nuclear arsenal. This would be a violation of the principle of irreversibility, the fifth of the steps agreed at the 2000 Review Conference. In order to adhere to its commitment to this principle, the UK must ensure that any successor system consists of fewer than 200 operationally available warheads, or if this is considered impossible for any reason, at the very least be prepared to explain in some detail why an increase in the number of warheads does not constitute an increase in the overall explosive power of the deterrent.

But this is not the only important constraint on the UK. It is not only the Non-Proliferation Treaty but also the Comprehensive Test Ban Treaty which must be taken into consideration, and this Treaty almost certainly limits the UK's possible options for any future deterrent. It is of course true that the Comprehensive Test Ban Treaty has not entered into force, and may quite possibly never do so, given that several of the states whose ratification is necessary for entry into force have not even signed it. But states which have ratified a Treaty are committed to abide by its provisions to the extent possible even without its entering into force. Moreover, even though the Treaty is not in force, there has for several years been an international moratorium on nuclear testing, which the United Kingdom would scarcely wish to be the first to violate. Finally, the UK has of course for many years had no test facilities of its own, and would therefore be unable to test, even if it wished to do so, without the agreement of (in practice) the United States.

While I did not at any time during my official career have detailed knowledge of these matters, it would seem to follow that for the future, the UK will be bound to stick to weapons designs which it has already tested. This would obviously severely limit the range of possibilities. Any idea that, in changed international circumstances, the UK could seek to configure its deterrent differently, perhaps to reduce costs, or to deal with different adversaries and threats from those faced during the Cold War, will inevitably run into this objection. It could in theory be argued that modern technology makes it possible to design nuclear weapons with a high degree of confidence without actually testing them to ensure their reliability. But I doubt whether weapons designers, military leaders, political leaders or public opinion would find this argument persuasive.

There is a further constraint which should also be borne in

mind in considering the case for acquiring a successor to Trident. It concerns the question of what the deterrent can be used to deter. Like the other recognized nuclear weapon states, the UK has given a so-called Negative Security Assurance regarding the possible use of its nuclear weapons against non-nuclear weapon states. Each of the five nuclear weapon states has stated its position in a slightly different form. The UK's negative security assurance was originally given in 1978, but was re-stated in the following somewhat different wording in 1995, at the time of the indefinite extension of the Non-Proliferation Treaty:

> The United Kingdom will not use nuclear weapons against non-nuclear weapon states party to the Treaty on the Non-Proliferation of Nuclear Weapons except in the case of an invasion or any other attack on the United Kingdom, its dependent territories, its armed forces or other troops, its allies or on a State towards which it has a security commit-ment, carried out or sustained by such a non-nuclear weapon state in association or alliance with a nuclear-weapon state. In giving this assurance the United Kingdom emphasises the need not only for universal adherence to, but also for compli-ance with, the Treaty . . . Her Majesty's Government does not regard its assurance as applicable if any beneficiary is in material breach of its own non-proliferation obligations under the Treaty.

This assurance was then repeated, together with those of the other recognized nuclear weapon states, in UN Security Council Resolution 984. The form of the Assurance makes it clear that it does not apply to two categories of non-nuclear weapon states – first, it does not apply to a non-nuclear weapon state which attacks the UK in alliance with a nuclear-weapon state; and second, it does not apply to one which has illegally acquired nuclear weapons or is seeking to acquire them, and has thus violated the NPT. But on the face of it, the Assurance does apply to a non-nuclear weapon state which possesses other weapons of mass destruction, i.e., biological and/or chemical weapons, even if those weapons were acquired in violation of commitments under the Biological and/or Chemical Weapons Conventions, and even if those weapons were used to attack the UK or UK forces. This contingency was probably not foreseen in 1978 when the Assurance was originally given, but it must certainly have been taken into account when the 1995 formulation was drawn up, because by that time the UK had been through the experience of the first Gulf War, when the threat that the Iraqi chemical and biological weapons might be used against British forces was taken very seriously.

Some of the other nuclear weapon states have in effect amended their negative security assurances to cover the point. For example, in 2002, after reiterating the negative security assurance of the United States, the official State Department spokesman went on: 'If a weapon of mass destruction is used against the United States or its allies, we will not rule out any specific type of military response.' At the 2005 NPT Review Conference, the French ambassador, likewise after re-stating France's negative security assurance, said: 'States that violate their non-proliferation commitments of course cannot claim protection under these assurances.' But even though from time to time UK ministers have sought to imply that Britain's response to an attack with chemical or biological weapons might be nuclear, the UK has not modified the terms of its Negative Security Assurance in any way. On 17 November 2003, Mr Dennis MacShane, a Foreign Office minister, said in a written parliamentary answer: 'The United Kingdom remains fully committed to the Negative Security Assurance we gave in 1995.' Ambassador David Broucher said in the 2004 statement to which I have already referred: 'The UK policy on Negative Security Assurances has not changed.' This point is obviously important because, unless the UK policy on Negative Security

Assurances is in fact changed, one of the arguments which might otherwise be adduced for maintaining and renewing the UK nuclear deterrent is deprived of its validity. It is important that this point should be addressed in the course of the overall debate on the future of the deterrent.

I conclude that the United Kingdom is not debarred by its commitments under the Non-Proliferation Treaty, or anything which has flowed from that Treaty, from replacing its existing nuclear capability, provided that it does not attempt to increase the size of its deterrent. However, the Comprehensive Test Ban Treaty does impose real constraints on the UK's options for a future generation of its deterrent. And the UK's Negative Security Assurance, unless amended, means that it would be inappropriate – indeed logically impossible – for the British government to argue that part of the case for replacing Trident would be the need to deter possible attacks on the UK forces using biological or chemical weapons.

If the United Kingdom were to decide on other grounds that it did not wish to retain its deterrent, then it would naturally seek to present the decision as a unique and unparalleled contribution to non-proliferation (which indeed it would be – no other recognized nuclear weapon state has renounced nuclear weapons, although South Africa gave up its existing nuclear capability in order to accede to the Non-Proliferation Treaty, and after the break-up of the Soviet Union, Belarus, Ukraine and Kazakhstan chose not to exercise the option of becoming nuclear weapon states by succession). However, opponents of the British deterrent tend to exaggerate the impact which such a decision might have. Just as it is hard to point to any other country which chose to develop nuclear weapons because Britain had done so, so it is hard to think of a country which would take the view that the termination of Britain's nuclear weapons capability meant that its own reasons for possessing nuclear weapons had thereby been removed, or even that in the light of the British decision, it could reduce its nuclear weapon holdings. The argument was famously used by Aneurin Bevan in 1957 that unilateral nuclear disarmament would mean sending a British Foreign Secretary 'naked into the conference chamber', and although this could scarcely nowadays be a decisive argument for the retention of the UK's nuclear weapon capability, it is probably still true, even at a time when the prospects for arms control do not look particularly good, that the UK's possession of nuclear weapons increases its ability to influence nuclear arms control negotiations, and thus, if it chooses to do so, to work for the implementation of Article VI.

# Technical Annex

The aim of this Annex is to describe the existing British Trident system covering the technical facts so far as they are publicly known, the dependence of the system on American support, and the options for maintaining a British deterrent system into the indefinite future.

## The existing British Trident system.

The Trident system consist of three principal components:

1 Four ballistic missile submarines: Vanguard, Victorious, Vigilant and Vengeance, built in Britain.
2 Fifty-eight Trident II (D5) missiles bought from the United States.
3 'Fewer than 200' operationally available nuclear warheads made in Britain.

### *The submarines*

The four submarines were built by Vickers Shipbuilding and Engineering Limited (now BAE Systems Marine) at Barrow in Furness and came into service between 1994 and 1999. They are based at HM Naval Base Clyde at Faslane and are refitted periodically at Devonport Royal Dockyard. This is owned and operated by a firm called DML in which the American firm Halliburton KBR owns a controlling interest of 51 per cent.[1] The boats are very large: 150 meters long and 12.8 metres wide, with a draught of 12 meters and displacement of 16,000 tonnes. They are equipped with 16 missile tubes for Trident D5 missiles. For self-defence they have four torpedo tubes for Spearfish homing torpedoes,[2] bow, flank and 'towed array' sonars, and collision avoidance radars. They have communication links to the Commander-in-Chief Fleet at Northwood, the Defence Secretary and the Prime Minister, so as to keep the use of the nuclear weapons under firm political control. The Trident boat is propelled by a Rolls Royce PWR2 (Pressurized Water Reactor) driving two GEC steam turbines, which give a submerged speed of 25 knots. It can travel great distances[3] and for many years without refuelling. It carries a crew of 17 officers and 134 ratings, all male. The accommodation is arranged on four decks and the messes serve not only as dining rooms but lecture halls, lounges, games areas and venues for church services. Members can receive short messages from home once a week, but since 'radio silence' has to be absolute these cannot be returned. Only one submarine is on deterrent patrol at any time, the average length of a patrol being between 70 and 80 days at sea. This submarine is normally at several days' notice to fire and its missiles are 'de-targeted'.[4] It can therefore carry out a variety of secondary tasks without compromising its security, including hydrographic data collection, equipment trials and exercises with other vessels.

## The missiles

Vanguard Class submarines are equipped to carry 16 Trident missiles. Britain has bought 58 Trident II (D5) missiles. These are either deployed on board the British submarines, or held ashore at Royal Naval Armament Depot Coulport (Loch Long) on a temporary basis, or in the US at the Strategic Weapons Facility Atlantic (Kings Bay, Georgia) as part of a shared pool of US/UK missiles. They are built by Lockheed Martin Space Systems at Sunnyvale, California. The missile is a three-stage, solid propellant, inertially guided missile, made of graphite epoxy. It is 44.5 feet long, 83 inches in diameter and weighs 58 tons. The range from submarine to target is given as 'over 4,000 nautical miles' and the time of flight, according to range, of up to 30 minutes. The launch from the submarine occurs under water. The missile is ejected from its tube using pressure created by a solid-fuel rocket motor attached to the bottom of the missile tube which heats a pool of water, creating steam. Ideally, the missile is sheathed in bubbles for its entire time submerged, so water never touches it. After the missile has left the water the first stage motor ignites, an aerospike[5] extends, and the boost stage begins. Within about two minutes, after the third stage motor fires, the missile is travelling faster than 6 km/s.[6] The missile carries a number of multiple independently targeted re-entry vehicles (MIRVs), each with a nuclear warhead. The D5 missile is designed to carry up to 12 MIRVs.[7] The missile's inertial system calculates flight trajectory and provides guidance. After the third rocket motor has separated, the warhead carrier (or Post Boost Vehicle – PBV) takes a sighting on two stars to confirm its position. Using gas generators and nozzles, the PBV aligns itself so as to dispatch the re-entry vehicles (RVs) in turn, each with its own point of aim.[8] Decoys and penetration aids, nested among the RVs, are also deployed at this stage.[9] All this takes place during the first one-third of the missile's trajectory. The RVs are not powered and the remaining two-thirds of their flight is ballistic (i.e. free-fall). They are cone shaped and fly at speeds between Mach 15 and 20 outside the atmosphere, slowing to Mach 10 during re-entry. Re-entry generates great heat which is absorbed by burning off the outer surface of the casing ('ablation'). The RVs are spun off their carrier by means of a small explosive charge. The spin maintains the correct attitude for re-entry and ensures that the casing cooks evenly during ablation. The accuracy of strike on target is given by the circle of equal probability (CEP), which is the radius of the circle within which half the strikes will impact. For

Trident D5 the CEP is given various values by different writers, lying between 100 and 500 m. The Royal Navy describes this as an 'accuracy that can be measured in metres' – which is undeniable.

## Target planning and fire control

Once a Trident submarine has launched a missile, its location has been compromised and it is in danger of attack. It follows that the classical mode of operation is a ripple launch in which all the missiles are discharged within about ten minutes. Since this could, in theory, involve 16 missiles each carrying 12 RVs (i.e. 192 different points of aim) the procedure is highly complex. Target planning takes place at the Nuclear Operations and Targeting Centre (NOTC) in London. Details for pre-arranged targets are supplied to the submarine on magnetic tape. Data can also be transmitted to the submarine by radio. The fire control system on the submarine receives the target data, updating the target database as necessary and assigns targets to missiles. It receives data on the exact position and speed of the submarine from the ship's inertial navigation system and navigational sonar.[10] It receives information on the strength and vertical deflection of gravity, both at the launch point and throughout the missile's trajectory, since this affects both the flight path of the missiles and the inertial navigation systems on the boat and the missiles.[11] It also needs information on the air density and wind speeds to be experienced by the RV during the final stages of its trajectory. It then allocates targets to RVs within the footprint of each missile, prepares the guidance system for each missile before launch, calculates the steering data for the missile and all its subordinate RVs and co-ordinates the launch sequence. At the last minute it sends an 'Intent Word' message to each missile. While in flight this message is communicated to each RV where it plays a crucial part in enabling the arming of the warhead. All this is performed on four computers networked together. The software is reported to contain more than one million lines of code. It has not been disclosed how long the process takes. A reasonable guess would be a few minutes for a single missile and a matter of a few hours for the whole boatload.

## Warheads

The UK Trident RV[12] is manufactured at the Atomic Weapons Establishment (AWE) at Aldermaston. AWE Management Limited is a joint venture company in which the American company Lockheed Martin has a one-third share. The warhead has been described as a 'Dutch Copy' of the American W76 warhead. This was manufactured in large numbers between 1978 and 1987 and deployed on D5 missiles. It has a yield of about 100 kilotons[13] and is the mainstay of the US nuclear deterrent system. A report in the Public Record Office says that the American design was 'anglicized' at Aldermaston.[14] The description that follows is based on the American W76 warhead except where stated. The RV consists of the Heatshield, the Arming, Fusing and Firing System (AF&F), the Nuclear Explosives Package (NEP) and two subsidiary components: the Neutron Generator and the Gas Transfer system, whose function will be described shortly.

The Heatshield, as already mentioned, is conical[15] and its function is to protect the warhead during re-entry by means of ablation. It is made of rayon-based carbon phenolics. Starting in 1977, Lockheed Martin built some 5,000 kits, including those for the British. The kits include the connectors to the Post Boost Vehicle and the release assembly which finally spins off the RV.

The Arming, Fusing and Firing System prepares the warhead for detonation in about a dozen separate steps controlled by a programming module. Its components include a battery, a timer and a radar that can detonate the warhead either as a high- or low-airburst. There is also a contact fuse. The system includes two safety links that can prevent detonation: an accelerometer to detect the launch of the missile and initiate the arming sequence; a decelerometer to detect a prescribed number of 'Gs' during re-entry and enable the warhead to be detonated. The Firing System supplies high-voltage power to initiate detonation and includes a ferroelectric firing set using a small amount of explosive to generate a pulse of high current, and a vacuum-tube switch that can very rapidly switch it on.

The Nuclear Explosives Package is the heart of the weapon. The system is a thermo-nuclear one, which means it contains two principal nuclear assemblies. The *Primary* is a spherical assembly that produces a fission yield through implosion. It consists of a series of concentric spherical shells. The outermost is made of high explosive and is detonated at a number of points simultaneously with the utmost precision, to ensure that the resultant inward shock wave is as spherical as possible. The innermost is a hollow sphere of about 4 kgs of plutonium – known by Americans as the 'pit'[16] – which under the intense pressure of the explosion contracts to form a supercritical mass and detonates by nuclear fission (i.e., as an atom bomb). Between these two layers is a shell of beryllium.[17] Its function is to contain the critical mass in the centre for as long as possible and to reflect back neutrons which have escaped from the exploding pit, thus lengthening and intensifying the explosive phase. Two other measures are taken to enhance this process. Just before the explosion, gaseous tritium is injected into the centre of the pit, boosting the yield by a fusion reaction. This is the function of the Gas Transfer system mentioned above. To start the detonation an ample supply of free neutrons is needed. The Neutron Generator, about the size of a beer can, fires a few instants after the high explosive to produce a flux of neutrons at the supercritical moment. All these events have to be accurately synchronized within a matter of nano-seconds.[18]

The *Secondary* is the fusion component of the weapon,

increasing its yield by a factor of about ten. Fusion takes place when light elements are exposed to extremely high temperatures, of the order of several 100 million degrees centigrade. This temperature is needed first to strip away the electrons from the atomic nuclei and then to overcome the natural charge repulsion of the nuclei themselves. It is almost impossible to achieve this for normal hydrogen but takes place more easily between two isotopes of hydrogen, deuterium and tritium.[19] If forced together, these nuclei fuse and then break apart to form a helium nucleus, a free neutron and a huge excess of energy. It happens that when lithium deuteride (a dry substance) is exposed to the neutron flux produced by a fission explosion it breaks up to produce free tritium. In the extreme heat of the fission explosion this tritium can fuse with the remaining deuterium in the lithium deuteride to produce the effects just described, so there is no need to include tritium separately. The fusion fuel in the Secondary is therefore normally a form of lithium deuteride. It is usually depicted as a column of fusion fuel. This is wrapped in a cylinder of unenriched uranium or lead[20] to help compress the fusion fuel, and inside it lies a hollow column of fissile fuel (plutonium or uranium-235). Due to its shape this is not originally a critical mass, but becomes so when the secondary detonates, thus adding to the power of the explosion.[21]

The *Radiation Case* is the metal cladding of the Nuclear Explosives Package. The primary and the secondary are immediately adjacent, and the crucial function of the Case is to channel radiation energy from the one to the other before the whole assembly is blown apart by blast. Since the duration of the entire process is measured in tens of nanoseconds, the importance of this function is self-evident.[22]

## The missile-warhead mix

The combination of missiles and warheads adopted for British Trident has never been revealed, except to say that the single submarine on deterrent patrol carries 48 operationally available nuclear warheads onboard.[23] Given the known characteristics of the system, and assuming that the missiles are uniformly loaded, this total could theoretically be made up in any one of five ways: sixteen missiles each with three warheads, twelve missiles each with four warheads, eight missiles each with six warheads, six missiles each with eight warheads or four missiles each with twelve warheads.[24] Most commentators give the standard load for British Trident missiles as four warheads (and by implication twelve missiles on the boat). This seems reasonable, lying well within the limiting numbers both for missiles and warheads and leaving plenty of room and payload on the post-boost vehicle for dummy warheads and penetration aids. However, it is unconfirmed. And a complication arose even before British Trident came into service. In the autumn of 1993 the then Defence Secretary Malcolm Rifkind announced a new role for the system resulting from the imminent renunciation of all British owned or operated tactical or 'theatre' nuclear weapons. He said that because against certain enemies the threat of an all-out nuclear assault might not be credible, it was important for Britain to be able to 'undertake a more limited nuclear strike' and so to deliver 'an unmistakable message of our willingness to defend our vital interests to the utmost'.[25] This is generally described as a 'sub-strategic' role. Although Rifkind said nothing about delivery, it has been generally assumed that this limited strike would be carried out by a missile carrying a single warhead, and there have been official statements seeming to corroborate this point.[26] Because the discharge of a single missile would compromise the location of the boat and render it vulnerable, it has been suggested that a 'second' vessel might be used, rather than the submarine on patrol.[27] And there have also been indications that this role could be more effectively carried out using a lower yield warhead.[28] There is no difficulty in principle with this suggestion. A yield of about ten kilotons could be obtained by replacing the secondary with an inert dummy of the same weight and inertial characteristics. A yield of about one kiloton could be achieved by additionally switching off the tritium gas injection system. However, it has been said that no additional costs have been incurred on account of the sub-strategic role,[29] which implies that no changes of any substance have been made to the hardware. It has also been explained that a missile with a single warhead could be used in either a strategic or sub-strategic attack.[30] This raises the possibility of other missile/warhead loadings for the submarine on patrol. Obvious combinations include eleven missiles with four warheads plus four missiles with single warheads. Or the total of 48 onboard warheads could be reduced.[31] These points are all moot. They are not, perhaps, of great importance. But the secrecy is clearly deliberate and it may well be that the Ministry of Defence is content if the flexibility and hence credibility of sub-strategic Trident is overestimated by the world at large.

## Dependence on the United States

At a meeting in Nassau, Bahamas in December 1962 between the US President Kennedy and British Prime Minister Macmillan it was agreed that the US would make available, on a continuing basis, ballistic missiles[32] (without warheads) for British submarines and certain support facilities for them. The Prime Minister undertook that these British forces would be used for the purposes of international defence of the Western alliance in all circumstances 'except where Her Majesty's Government may decide that supreme national interests are at stake'.[33] Since then the United Kingdom has committed all its nuclear forces, both strategic, and sub-strategic, to NATO.[34]

Four years previously, under the Mutual Defence Agreement of 1958, the US agreed to sell to Britain a complete submarine nuclear propulsion plant, the necessary information to design, manufacture and operate such a plant and sufficient enriched uranium fuel for ten years of operation. In an amendment the following year the US agreed to supply Britain with non-nuclear parts of atomic weapons systems, together with 'special nuclear material'[35] required for research, development or manufacture of atomic weapons where the transfer of such material was necessary to improve the United Kingdom's capability in these areas. The UK would transfer to the US similar materials for military purposes.[36] This arrangement has been recently extended, by agreement between the President and the Prime Minister, for a further ten years until December 2014.[37] These agreements have underpinned the close and continuing link between the two countries in constructing, operating and maintaining the British strategic nuclear submarine force over the past 40 years.

## The submarine, its communications and navigation systems

The Trident submarines have been built in Britain to British designs though based in part, no doubt, on the design of the American Trident Submarines, the Ohio Class.[38] The original reactor design came from America, as explained above, but since then British submarine reactors have developed on separate lines. Rolls Royce and associates have developed a new fuel core for British submarines which has been on test at HMS *Vulcan*, Dounreay, for the past five years and is being installed on Trident submarines as they come up for refit. These cores run on uranium enriched to around 98 per cent. According to a 1997 press release the UK had received from America some 7.5 tonnes of enriched uranium over the years, in exchange for some 5.4 tonnes of plutonium.[39]

Secure radio communications are essential for these submarines. They are also problematic, because raising an antenna above the water can lead to early detection. A submarine can receive signals, without having to do this, in the radio bands known as Low Frequency (LF) or Very Low Frequency (VLF). A new VLF transmitter at Skelton, near Penrith, operated by VT Merlin Communications, is the primary means of communicating with British Trident submarines.[40] The same firm is supplying new VLF receivers for the boats. There is also a NATO VLF network, with transmitters at Anthorn, Cumbria and in Norway, Germany and Italy. America also has a VLF/LF network with transmitters in the US and in Puerto Rico, Iceland and Italy, primarily to communicate with US Navy Trident submarines in the Atlantic. This network now provides channels compatible with NATO and hence with the UK. A NATO-wide code for transmitting data is now in use. There is also a bi-lateral system allowing the US Trident Commander at King's Bay, Georgia to communicate directly with British Trident Submarines.

To communicate with satellites the submarines have to raise their antennae above water for a few minutes. Even then there are problems of low bandwidth. British submarines have access to British, NATO and US satellite systems, operating in the Ultra High Frequency (UHF) and Super High Frequency (SHF) bands. In nuclear war these satellites might have been disabled by high altitude nuclear bursts.[41] The US is accordingly introducing a new Extremely High Frequency (EHF) system for strategic nuclear forces. British EHF communications will rely on the use of an American satellite. New shore-based terminals will then provide 'robust, high data-rate satellite communications to British submarines'. But this system is apparently not being fitted to Vanguard Class submarines.[42]

Navigation is also a major concern, since knowing the submarine's exact position is critical to accurate targeting. Four systems are used:

1 The Global Positioning Satellite (GPS) system, which was specifically designed to provide navigational fixes for submarines. It is owned and operated by the US, and the British have to use the same system, at least until such time as the European Galileo system goes live in a few years' time.[43] GPS is extremely accurate, but the signals cannot be received under water. Raising the aerial risks compromising the submarine and the satellites may not survive in a nuclear war.

2 Between GPS fixes the boat's position is tracked by an inertial system – using gyroscopes to record direction and accelerometers to record distances moved. The British use the same system as the Americans but could, at a pinch, devise their own.

3 Navigational Sonar Systems measure the speed of the submarine over the sea-bed and the depth of water under the boat. The latter is compared with a map of the sea-bed to help fix the submarine's position. It is not known what type of navigational sonar is used on British Trident submarines.

4 Mapping. This is crucial to Trident operations for two reasons: first, to help in navigation as just mentioned, and second, because of the importance of gravitational data in computing the flight path of the missiles as explained earlier. The US Navy has surveyed small areas in detail to support Trident operations, under its Ocean Survey Programme.[44] Their submarines on deterrent patrol operate only in these areas, using map data provided in digital form. Their location and the related data are therefore highly classified. The British hydrographic ship HMS *Scott* is equipped to provide data in a format compatible with the American system. No doubt British submarines patrol in areas surveyed by this ship. It is not known whether patrol area data is exchanged with the Americans. If not, this must severely limit the choice of areas for the British.

## The missiles and their targeting

The D5 missiles used on British Trident are American. The hardware and much of the software associated with their targeting and firing are also of American provenance. The 58 missiles 'bought' by the UK are not British exclusive property but form part of a 'shared pool of US/UK missiles'[45] based on the Strategic Weapons Facility Atlantic at Kings Bay, Georgia.[46] The weapons are collected from there by British submarines and returned there for refurbishment as necessary. During the commissioning of each British submarine, and after each major overhaul, an unarmed missile is fired, under American supervision, at the US Eastern Test Range, Cape Canaveral,[47] and the missile flight data are analysed to assess reliability and accuracy at Johns Hopkins University Applied Physics Laboratory at Laurel, Maryland.[48]

Hardware for the Fire Control System (FCS) on Trident submarines is produced by the American firm General Dynamics Defence Systems. It has recently been upgraded to allow for more rapid re-targeting of missiles and to incorporate more commercially replaceable components. The new FCS entered service on British Trident submarines during the winter 2002/3.[49] It appears to be very similar to that being introduced on the American boats. Software for this system is developed by a division of the Naval Surface Warfare Centre at Dahlgren, Virginia. This software has also been upgraded recently. Again there is good reason to suppose that the British version is almost identical to the American. For example, a contract was let in 2002 to the firm CACI[50] at Arlington, Virginia, for software testing and support for the Trident FCS, of which the UK will pay a 10 per cent share,[51] and in April 2005 the US Navy won a contract for 'UK Intent Word Displays' for the British system.[52] The software for the computers in the British Targeting Centre, NOTC, is also based on American models.

Given that the Royal Navy uses American software for target

planning, data handling and fire control, it has been suggested that these programs might have been doctored to require approval by US Strategic Command (STRATCOM) before they will work. It is even possible that, hidden among the million or so lines of code in the Fire Control System, a few lines might have been inserted to restrict target locations within particular bounds: for example to rule out an attack on the United States, or on Russia, unless authorized by the US. There is no evidence that anything like this has ever been done. But it is possible; and if it were done then the British might never spot it.

## Warheads

As the AWE Annual Report for 2004 explains, co-operation with the US on nuclear weapon matters, under the 1958 Mutual Defence Agreement, 'covers every aspect of weapon design, development and maintenance'.[53] So no one doubts the description of the British Trident warhead, quoted earlier, as an American W76 warhead 'anglicized' at Aldermaston. It is generally assumed that all the items of the Re-entry Vehicle outside the Nuclear Explosives Package are of American supply. The Heatshield kits, as already explained, were made by Lockheed Martin. The Arming, Fusing and Firing (AF&F) Systems for the British warhead were designed by Sandia National Laboratories, and are almost certainly bought from the United States as a package. A new Neutron Generator was designed and built between 1997 and 2002, and first units were supplied to the British in 2003.[54] The Gas Transfer System is also American. Because Tritium gas is radioactive and can penetrate stainless steel it requires special reservoirs. Because it decays to produce helium, thus increasing the pressure in the reservoirs, it has to be replaced regularly. British tritium is transported to America as uranium tritide, converted to tritium gas and loaded into reservoirs at the Savannah River site. Both the Neutron Generators and the Gas Transfer System, being limited life items, are replaced on a regular basis. This is done in the Re-entry Body Process Building at Coulport, before the warheads are fitted to the missiles on board the submarines.

The Nuclear Explosives Package is designed and made at Aldermaston. One difference from the American system is that the British use a different high explosive.[55] No doubt design data were regularly exchanged with the Americans, and live testing of British warheads, while this was allowed, took place in Nevada.[56] But that does not detract from the British ability to design and build the Nuclear Explosive Package as it exists today.

### Can British Trident operate independently of the US?

Under the Mutual Defence Agreement of 1958, co-operation by either party is contingent on its determining that such action 'will promote and will not constitute an unreasonable risk to its defence and security'. The message is clear that such co-operation could be withdrawn at any time if the UK embarked on a course of action that the US regarded as inimical to its interests. The agreement referred to the fact that the two countries were participating in an international arrangement for their mutual defence and security (i.e. NATO) and at Nassau the British Prime Minister agreed that the strategic missiles to be provided would be used for the nuclear defence of the alliance. It follows that planning for the use of UK Trident is closely co-ordinated both with the American STRATCOM in Omaha and with NATO. A British liaison cell is maintained at STRATCOM.[57] The senior US officer in Europe, who is also the NATO commander (SACEUR), allocates targets for British nuclear weapons. The British Commander-in-Chief Fleet is also Commander of Allied Naval Forces North. He exercises operational command of Trident from his headquarters at Northwood, Middlesex. It follows that, so long as British Trident is operated within the NATO context, whether strategically or sub-strategically, no conflict of interest is likely to arise. The question remains whether British Trident could be used without the United States' consent and assistance and could be targeted independently of US assistance. When this question was put in the House of Lords in 1995 the government spokesman replied, 'Trident is an independent nuclear deterrent. That means exactly that, I can go no further.'[58] The Delphic nature of this response is obviously deliberate.

The issue needs to be discussed at two different levels. If the US were to determine that co-operation on British Trident was no longer promoting American defence and security, or was posing an unreasonable risk to it, then all technical assistance could be withdrawn. Denied help in maintaining, testing and upgrading the missiles, the fire control system and key components of the warhead, and with no re-supply of life restricted items for the latter (tritium injection system and neutron generator) the whole system would start to become unworkable and probably unsafe within a matter of a year or so. The UK has had no capacity to design and build a missile of strategic range since the demise of the liquid-fuelled Blue Streak in 1960. To re-create such a capacity would take a decade and the expense would be astronomical. Shopping around for another foreign supplier (Russia, China, North Korea) would be very unattractive, and there would still be the difficulty of fitting the submarines and warheads to match the new missiles. No wonder the British Prime Minister is at pains to stay on the right side of the American administration where major issues of peace and war are concerned.

Assuming that the system remains functional, there remains the question of actually firing a missile in circumstances where the Americans were either neutral or actively opposed. The submarine could presumably be sailed to an area where the sea-bed had been accurately surveyed. The order to fire could be conveyed and authenticated by VLF radio without the submarine either raising an antenna or using an American satellite. The missile would then presumably work, although the accuracy might be impaired if gravitational and weather information, normally supplied by the Americans, was not available. The unsettling possibility has already been discussed that the software for fire control or in the warhead fusing system might have been secretly doctored so as to require independent US authorization to fire. It is also just conceivable that the Americans, bearing in mind historic suspicions of small independent forces,[59] could have inserted duff components anyway. But these suppositions hardly deserve serious consideration. The reasonable conclusion is that if the British Prime Minister, getting the bit between his teeth, deciding that 'supreme national interests were at stake', regardless of the nuclear taboo and the likely reaction of the entire world (not least the USA), were to order Trident to fire, then it would do so. Short of attacking the submarine, the communication centre at Skelton or the Prime Minister, there is nothing the Americans could do to stop it.

## Future options

The 2005 election manifesto of the present British Labour government made clear its commitment to maintaining the UK's 'independent nuclear deterrent'. In amplification the Defence Secretary John Reid has said that a decision will have to be taken in the life of this Parliament (i.e., by 2010 at the latest) whether to 'modify, replace, update or diminish Trident'.[60] This section sets out some of the technical considerations involved in that decision.

Tim Hare, former Director for Nuclear Policy in the MoD, has argued forcefully that 'more of the same' is the only realistic answer.[61] In his opinion, the argument for staying with a submarine-launched Trident system is overwhelming, not only on grounds of the operational advantages of stealth and invulnerability,[62] but equally on grounds of cost. This means keeping the existing system going as long as possible and then replacing it with something as similar as possible – no doubt following the Americans all the way. Such a policy would fit comfortably with the terms set out by the Defence Secretary for updating, modifying or replacing Trident, probably in that order. The implications of this policy fall differently as between the submarines, the missiles and the warheads. We consider these in turn.

The official life of the British Vanguard class submarines is 25 years. On this basis the first submarine would retire in 2019 and the last in 2024. But compared with normal submarines, Trident boats typically operate at somewhat shallower depths, do not experience nearly as many excursions from their normal operating depth, and would not operate below their test depth with any degree of frequency. So it could be expected that they would experience less 'fatigue' and could have a longer operating life than attack submarines. The US Navy now assumes that their Ohio-class submarines will have an operating lifetime of at least 42 years: two 20-year operating cycles separated by a two-year refuelling overhaul.[63] An obvious move would be to extend the life of British Trident submarines accordingly: i.e., until 2046 to 2051. One critical factor would be the life of the reactor core. Ohio completed 22 years on its first fuel core. The new British fuel core, of which a prototype is being tested at Dounreay, is designed to last 25 years. The predicted life will be adjusted in the light of this test, from inspections during refits and from HMS *Vanguard*'s second visit to Devonport scheduled for 2012. The life of the hull is also critical. Hull and reactor problems affected British Polaris submarines during their later years and there have been a number of serious reactor defects recently on nuclear-powered attack submarines. If the life of British submarines cannot safely be extended, it will be necessary to build new boats. It has been announced that both options are being studied.[64]

The Americans have a life extension programme for D5 missiles, with an upgraded guidance system extending their life by 15 years until 2042. The British have apparently no plans at present to acquire the upgraded missiles, but there is no reason in principle why they should not negotiate to acquire these by a further amendment to the Mutual Defence Agreement – at a price.

The largest element of the American nuclear weapons programme is a project to upgrade the W76 warhead. The resulting warheads (W76-1) are due to enter service between 2008 and 2013, with a planned life of 30 years to match the new lifespan of the submarines and missiles. Most of the British warheads were delivered to the Coulport depot between 1993 and 1998. Since the life of the high explosive is probably about 12 years, a refurbishment programme is presumably under way, designed to match the original planned life of the British boats. After that a re-design might well be needed, in line no doubt with the American W76-1, and Aldermaston has carefully nurtured a design team to cope with this requirement.[65]

As regards 'diminishing Trident', there should be no difficulty. Under the more relaxed post-Cold War conditions, a fleet of three boats might be sufficient. The rationale for keeping a stock of 58 missiles and 'under 200' operationally available warheads has never been explained, other than to say it is the 'minimum necessary to deter any threat to our vital interests'.[66] As discussed earlier, there would be no difficulty in operating a submarine on deterrent patrol with fewer than eight missiles on board and fewer than four warheads on each.[67] Although this might not save much money, this would enable the British government to demonstrate further progress towards nuclear disarmament, as treaty commitments require.

One possible alternative to Trident would be to acquire the American sea-launched cruise missile in its nuclear version, Tomahawk Land Attack Missile – Nuclear (TLAM–N). Conventionally armed versions of the same missile were fired from submarines and surface ships in attacks on Iraq, Afghanistan, Serbia and Sudan. Britain deploys these conventional missiles on some submarines and plans to equip all attack submarines with them in due course. TLAM–N was introduced into the American fleet in the 1980s[68] and it has been suggested that Britain might deploy them on Astute class submarines as an alternative to Trident. This would involve a huge reduction in firepower in comparison with Trident, the purchase of a new missile system, a new design of warhead and support facilities and no doubt heavy costs.[69] Moreover there is every sign that the US Navy is unenthusiastic about TLAM–N and may shortly begin to phase them out.

A third alternative would be to transfer the nuclear strategic role back to the RAF, perhaps by fitting a nuclear warhead to missiles carried on the new Typhoon aircraft. In the 1980s Britain had considered such a project as a tactical weapon instead of free-fall bombs. One possibility was to acquire the American missile known as Short Range Attack Missile – Tactical (SRAM–T) which was to use an existing nuclear warhead. Another idea was to combine with the French, using their missile Air-Sol Longue Portée (ASLP). In the early 1990s both these projects were cancelled, but not before a British warhead had been designed for this purpose.[70] At present there is no American project on these lines and the prospect of a go-it-alone British version is all but negligible.

It seems, therefore, that Tim Hare's view is likely to be vindicated, subject only to a plan being devised at an acceptable cost. With programmes for future aircraft carriers, new frigates and Astute Class submarines all in the pipeline the naval budget will be under unusual stress in the near future. Much will depend on the price tags that emerge from present studies, and until these are available further speculation is unprofitable.[71] The position was neatly summed up by Admiral Sir Alan West in an interview given just before he retired as First Sea Lord. He said,

We don't need a new deterrent as such, because the Trident missile has along life ahead of it and we have already made significant investment in the supporting infrastructure. What we will need are new submarines to replace the Vanguard class and I think now is the time to start design work on that next deterrent boat if we are to maintain the minimum deterrent.[72]

## Acknowledgement

The writer acknowledges his debt to the research carried out by John Ainslie for his Report 'The Future of the British Bomb'. Material from that report, and more particularly references, are to be found on every page of this Annex. To acknowledge these ascriptions individually would be vexatious so this more general acknowledgement must suffice.

# Notes

## Introduction

1 http://www.cathnews.com/news/511/91.php. In discussion with the editor, David Ryall from the staff of the Bishops' Conference for England and Wales has pointed out that the Catholic Church's analysis of the morality of nuclear weapons is perhaps the most developed of any religious tradition and includes not only the reflections by the Holy See but also the extensive literature produced by national bishops' conferences, especially in the United States, France, Germany, Scotland, and England and Wales. Pope John Paul II, in his June 1982 statement to the UN Special Session on disarmament and his January 1988 address to the diplomatic corps accredited to the Holy See, and the US bishops' 1983 pastoral *The Challenge of Peace: God's Promise and Our Response* remain key documents within that still developing body of moral teaching. Part of the richness of the Catholic tradition in this area is the way in which discussions of the nuclear question are placed within a much broader framework of human ends and values and the nature of political community.

2 See D. Fisher, *Morality and the Bomb*, London: Croom Helm; New York: St Martin's Press, 1985, pp. 43–4.

3 The reader may wish to look at the correspondence between Fisher and Wicker on the CCADD website at: http://www.lineone.net/~ccadd under 'documents'.

4 See below, p. 97.

## Chapter 1

1 Helmut Thielicke, *Theological Ethics, Vol. II*, London: A. and C. Black, 1968.

2 Richard Harries, *Christianity and War in a Nuclear Age*, London: Mowbray, 1986, pp. 76–144.

3 *Countering Terrorism: Power, Violence and Democracy Post 9/11*, report of a working party of the House of Bishops, Church House Bookshop, 31 Great Smith Street, London SW1 P3BN.

4 *Christianity and War in a Nuclear Age*, chapter 2.

5 *Countering Terrorism*, pp. 32–4.

## Chapter 2

1 CAB 80/94: COS(45)402(o), Future Development in Weapons and Methods of War, 16 June 1945.

2 CAB 21/2093: 19/10/201, The Basis of Service Estimates, 9 January 1931.

## Chapter 3

1 This chapter has been reproduced, with the author's kind permission, from an address to the US Catholic Bishops' Panel on 'Ethics, Policy and the Proliferation of WMD' given in Washington DC on 11 November 2005.

## Chapter 4

1 David Fisher, *Morality and the Bomb*, London: Croom Helm; New York: St Martin's Press, 1985.

2 The just-war conditions are so described in Fisher, *Morality and the Bomb*, chapters 2–3.

3 Michael Clarke, 'Does my bomb look big in this? Britain's nuclear choices after Trident', *International Affairs*, Vol. 80, 2004, p. 59.

4 David S. Yost, 'France's evolving nuclear Strategy', *Survival*, The IISS Quarterly, Vol. 47, No. 3, Autumn 2005, pp. 117–47.

5 Michael Clarke, for example, argues in 'Does my bomb look big in this?', p. 61, that 'All the major trends in the world that the UK faces up to 2030 – trends that defence officials are publicly trying to think through – suggest that the changes of the last decade or so are systemic rather than short term.'

6 J. M. Finnis, J. M. Boyle Jr and G. Grisez, *Nuclear Deterrence, Morality and Realism*, Oxford: Clarendon Press, 1987.

7 Jacques Chirac, speech at the Institut des Hautes Études de Défense National, 8 June 2001, quoted in Yost, p. 118. President Chirac expanded further on the theme of the need for more employable and discriminate nuclear options in his speech in January 2006 reported in David S. Yost, 'France's new nuclear doctrine', *International Affairs*, Vol 82, no. 4, July 2006, pp. 701–21.

8 Henri Bentégeat, evidence to Commission de la Défense Nationale at des Forces Armées, 13 November 2002, quoted in Yost, p. 120.

9 Henri Bentégeat, interview in *Jane's Defence Weekly*, 4 June 2003.

# Notes

*Chapter 5*

1 Lee Butler, Commander in Chief of US Strategic Air Command 1991–2, 'At the end of a journey: The risks of Cold War thinking in a new era', in *Alternative Nuclear Futures*, ed. John Baylis and Robert O'Neill, Oxford University Press, 2000, p. 189.

2 This is argued at length and in detail by John Finnis, Joseph M. Boyle and Germain Grisez in *Nuclear Deterrence, Morality and Realism*, Oxford University Press, 1987, on whose arguments I rely fairly heavily in this article (subsequently referred to as: Finnis and Co). Some of the arguments put in this chapter are stated more fully in my 'Nuclear pacifism in the post-Cold War world', in *Demanding Peace: Christian Responses to War and Violence*, ed. Anthony Harvey, London: SCM Press, 1999, pp. 106–41.

3 In 1968 Secretary of Defense Robert McNamara judged that destroying 20–25 per cent of the Soviet population and 50 per cent of its industrial capacity would serve as an effective deterrent (figures quoted by Sir Arthur Hockaday in G. L. Goodwin (ed.), *Ethics and Nuclear Deterrence*, London: Croom Helm, 1982, p. 72). Although considered by Hockaday a gross inflation of what is necessary, the figure gives some indication of what some people in the past considered appropriate for effective deterrence.

4 Barrie Paskins, in Goodwin, *Ethics and Nuclear Deterrence*, p. 99.

5 On this, see G. E. M. Anscombe, *Intention*, Oxford: Basil Blackwell, 1st edn, 1957, section 22.

6 Finnis and Co., pp. 92ff.

7 After the Nazi atrocity at Lidice, Churchill was adamant that the Allies should deliberately wipe out German villages in retaliation, and was only dissuaded by Clement Attlee, (see *The Guardian*, 2 January 2006, reporting on newly released notebooks of the Cabinet Secretary Sir Norman Brooks). A. C. Grayling, in *Among the Dead Cities*, Bloomsbury, 2006, recounts in chapter 2 the process whereby an initial policy of not targeting civilian areas in the Second World War turned into a plan for the wholesale destruction of German cities and their populations. An example of the difficulty of avoiding civilian casualties even when they are not intended is illustrated by recently released documents about the bombing of Rome in 1943, which took place despite opposition from the Vatican and Cardinal Hinsley. Not surprisingly, while supposedly aiming at the railway marshalling yards, a church was hit and many people killed (*The Tablet*, 31 December 2005, p. 17). Clearer still is the example of the 'flattening' of Cleves in order to make the crossing of the Rhine safer for Allied troops – an action which gave the British general in charge grave misgivings. (Quoted by Duncan

Forrester in *Apocalypse Now? Reflections on Faith in a Time of Terror*, Aldershot: Ashgate, 2005, p. 93).

8  Finnis and Co., pp. 92ff.

9  *Sunday Times*, 19 June 2005.

10  This phrase is given further confirmation by a report of what Richard Nixon said during the Watergate affair: 'I can go into the next room and pick up the phone and 25 minutes later 75 million people will be dead' (Elaine Scarry, in *The Guardian*, 'The ideas interview', 7 November 2005).

11  Oliver Kamm, in this book, points out with approval that 'most people in Britain . . . lose no sleep over the mass annihilation that our Trident fleet could unleash'. This is doubtless true; but majority opinion is no test of ethical truth.

12  As far as warfare is concerned, perhaps Clausewitz's opening dismissal of 'self-imposed, imperceptible limitations hardly worth mentioning' on the practice of warfare, such as international law and custom, mark the modern turning-point towards a consequentialist view of war and its morality. For discussion of some consequentialist just-war arguments for permitting nuclear deterrence, see Finnis and Co., pp. 177ff. In her celebrated essay on 'Modern Moral Philosophy' G. E. M. Anscombe decisively refuted modern forms of consequentialist ethics (G. E. M. Anscombe, *Collected Philosophical Papers*, Oxford: Basil Blackwell, 1981, Vol. III, pp. 26–42). This essay marked the start of a turn away from consequentialism towards the return to ethics as the study of the virtues.

13  See Herbert McCabe OP, 'Politics and virtue', in *The Good Life*, Continuum, 2005. See also Jean Porter, *Nature as Reason: A Thomistic Theory of the Natural Law*, Grand Rapids: Wm B. Eerdmans, 2005.

14  See the correspondence between Brian Wicker and David Fisher on the CCADD website at: http://website.lineone.net/~ccadd under 'documents: correspondence'.

15  Anscombe, *Modern Moral Philosophy*, p. 35.

16  Hockaday, *Ethics and Nuclear Deterrence*, p. 85, and Anscombe, *Modern Moral Philosophy*, p. 33 note.

17  Carl von Clausewitz, *On War*, ed. and trans. Michael Howard and Peter Paret, Princeton University Press, 1984, chapter 1, p. 75.

18  See Finnis and Co., chapter VI, sections 2, 4 and 5.

19  See *Sunday Telegraph*, 16 October 2005.

20  Finnis and Co., Chapter VI, section 2; and see note 7 above. Paul Rogers has pointed out that any attack on Iran's nuclear facilities, many of which are in cities, would cause thousands of civilian deaths. See *Iran: Consequences of a War*, Oxford Research Group, 2006; and *The Guardian*, 13 February 2006.

21 Al-Qaeda's 'ethic' is of course thoroughly consequentialist. A particularly blatant illustration of this appeared in a letter sent in July 2005 to its commander in Iraq, Abu Musab al-Zarqawi, telling him to shoot rather than behead hostages 'because brutal executions alienate the Muslim world' (Report by Rory Carroll from Baghdad in *The Guardian*, 8 October 2005).

22 Elsewhere I have argued this point in more detail, albeit before the advent of al-Qaeda-type terrorism and the events of 9/11. See 'When is a war not a war?' and 'From national to international policing' in *Some Corner of a Foreign Field: Intervention and World Order*, ed. Roger Williamson for the Council on Christian Approaches to Defence and Disarmament, Basingstoke: Macmillan Press, 1998, pp. 38–47 and 107–17. The rise of global terrorism only makes the argument I propose there stronger and more urgent. Too much of the argument for Britain's retention of nuclear weapons rests on a dubious assumption that the current division of humankind into competing sovereign states is permanent and unalterable, whereas in reality it is neither.

23 This judgement is confirmed by the latest condemnation of nuclear deterrence by the Pope. In his New Year Peace-day message for 1 January 2006, Benedict XVI asks: 'What can be said about those governments which count on nuclear arms as a means of ensuring the security of their countries? Along with countless persons of good will, one can state that this point of view is not only baneful but also completely fallacious . . . the truth of peace requires that all – whether those governments which openly or secretly possess nuclear arms, or those planning to acquire them – agree to change their course by clear and firm decisions, and strive for a progressive and concerted nuclear disarmament.'

## Chapter 6

1 'What did CND achieve?', *The Guardian*, 6 August 2002.

2 'We must use unilateral steps taken by Britain to secure multilateral solutions on the international level. Unilateralism and multilateralism must go hand in hand if either is to succeed', *Labour Party Manifesto 1983: New Hope for Britain*.

3 Reinhold Niebuhr, *Love and Justice: Selections from the Later Writings of Reinhold Niebuhr*, New York: Westminster John Knox Press, 1972, p. 59.

4 Graham S. Pearson, *The Search for Iraq's Weapons of Mass Destruction: Inspection, Verification and Non-Proliferation*, Basingstoke: Palgrave Macmillan, 2005, pp. 229–30.

5 Colin S. Gray, *The Sheriff: America's Defence of the New World*

*Order*, Lexington, Kentucky: University of Kentucky Press, 2004, p. 76.

## Chapter 7

1 There are similarities between Suez and our assault on Iraq. Both were notable for flouting UN authority, for deceptive decision-making by an over-confident Prime Minister, and for the failure to achieve the expedition's stated objective. A major difference is that, after Suez, it only took five months to clear up the mess and re-open the Canal. In Iraq, we are three years down the road and still counting.

2 There would have been no Gulf War in 1991 if Washington had made it crystal clear to Iraq that it would respond with overwhelming military force to any aggression against Kuwait by Iraq. Nor would Argentina have invaded the Falklands if there had been no doubt that we would respond forcefully.

3 Incidentally, France signed the Non Proliferation Treaty only in 1992, seeing the Treaty as an attempt by the Anglo-Saxons to corner the market in nuclear exports.

4 See *Disarmament Diplomacy* No. 77, May–June 2004, p. 23.

## Chapter 9

1 Charles Lindblom, *The Policy-making Process*, Prentice Hall, 1968.

2 Daniel Kahneman and Amos Tversky, 'Judgment under uncertainty: heuristics and biases', in *Science*, 185, 1974, pp. 1124–31.

3 For a more extensive description of this model, see Tom Sauer, *Nuclear Inertia: US Nuclear Weapons Policy After the Cold War*, I. B. Tauris, 2005, esp. chapter 7.

4 In case voters have no expectations, they will certainly not speak out.

5 H. Beach *et al.*, 'An end to UK nuclear weapons?', in *British Pugwash Paper*, 2002, p. 25, quoted in Michael Clarke, 'Does my bomb look big in this? Britain's nuclear choices after Trident', in *International Affairs*, Vol. 80, No. 1, January 2004, p. 53.

6 Michael Portillo, 'Does Britain need nuclear missiles? No. Scrap them', in *The Times*, 19 June 2005.

7 *Missile Defence: A Public Discussion Paper*, British Ministry of Defence, December 2002, par. 68, quoted in David Yost, 'New approaches to deterrence in Britain, France, and the United States', in *International Affairs*, Vol. 81, No. 1, 2005, p. 103.

8 They all signed either the Generals Statement against Nuclear Weapons in 1996 or the Civilians' Statement against Nuclear Weapons

in 1998.

9 Ken Booth, 'Nuclear weapons: Britain's role in the transition from MAD to a SANE world', in *ISIS Special Report*, September 1997.

10 Michael MccGwire, 'Is there a future for nuclear weapons?' in *International Affairs*, Vol. 70, No. 2, 1994, pp. 211–28; Michael MccGwire, 'The rise and fall of the NPT: an opportunity for Britain', in *International Affairs*, Vol. 81, No. 1, 2005, pp. 115–40.

11 Clarke, 'Does my bomb look big in this?'.

12 Paul Williams, *The Al Qaeda Connection*, Prometheus Books, 1995.

13 'El Baradei warns of potential for 30 nuclear powers', in *NTI Global Security Newswire*, 14 December 2005.

14 Portillo, 'Does Britain need nuclear missiles?'.

15 Already in the beginning of 2006, there were rumours that the British Atomic Weapons Establishment had plans to hire an additional 1,000 scientists and engineers, raising concerns that the decision to modernize the British nuclear weapons arsenal had already been taken. See Colin Brown, 'Hiring of scientists creates fear of nuclear programme', in *The Independent*, 15 March 2006.

16 Robin Cook, 'Worse than irrelevant', in *The Guardian*, 29 June 2005.

17 McNamara, interviewed by Jonathan Schell, 'The gift of time', in *The Nation*, 2 February 1998, p. 26.

18 Tom Sauer, *Nuclear Inertia*, esp. chapters 9–11; Janne Nolan, *An Elusive Consensus. Nuclear Weapons and American Security after the Cold War*, Brookings Institution, 1999.

19 'We will work to create conditions in which even a minimum level of nuclear deterrence is no longer necessary', *The Strategic Defence Review: Supporting Essays*, par. 55, 1998.

20 Richard Neustadt, *Thinking in Time: The Use of History for Decision-makers*, Free Press, 1988.

21 Quoted in *Arms Control and Security Letter*, No. 12 (156), PIR Center, Moscow, December 2004.

22 Cook, 'Worse than irrelevant'.

23 MoD White Paper, December 2003, quoted by Richard Norton-Taylor, 'A most dangerous message', in *The Guardian*, 13 April 2005. See also Marc Millot, 'Facing the emerging reality of regional nuclear proliferation', in *The Washington Quarterly*, Summer 1994.

24 Michael Quinlan, 'The future of nuclear weapons in world affairs', in *The Bulletin of the Atlantic Council of the US*, 20 November 1996, p. 2.

25 Paul Nitze, 'A conventional approach', in *Proceedings*, May 1994, p. 46.

26 Michael Quinlan, 'It is crucial to enhance deterrence', in *Financial Times*, 16 March 2005.

27 Michael MccGwire, 'The rise and fall of the NPT', 2005, p. 131.

*Chapter 10*

1 Ira B. Nadel, *Various Positions: A Life of Leonard Cohen*, London: Bloomsbury, 1996, p. 261.

2 Martin Amis, *Einstein's Monsters,* Author's note and Introduction: thinkability, London: Jonathan Cape, 1987.

3 Ted Post (Director), *Beneath the Planet of the Apes*, film by 20th Century Fox, 1970.

4 Working Party of the Board for Social Responsibility of the General Synod of the Church of England. *Peacemaking in a Nuclear Age*, London: Church House Publishing, 1988, pp. 32–3, 163, 174.

5 Working party, under the chairmanship of the Bishop of Salisbury, set up by the General Synod of the Church of England. *The Church and the Bomb: Nuclear Weapons and Christian Conscience*. London: CIO Publishing, Hodder and Stoughton, 1982, p. 125.

6 Paul Ramsey, *Who Speaks for the Church?*, Edinburgh: St Andrews Press, 1969.

7 Barbara Victor, *The Last Crusade: Religion and the Politics of Misdirection*, London: Constable, 2005.

8 Jonathan Schell, *The Gift of Time: The Case for Abolishing Nuclear Weapons Now*, London: Granta Books, 1998, p. x and quote from Joseph Rotblat, p. 58.

9 Robert Hinde and Joseph Rotblat, *War No More: Eliminating Conflict in the Nuclear Age*, London: Pluto Press, 2003, p. 5.

10 Robert McNamara, *Out of the Cold: New Thinking for American Foreign and Defence Policy in the 21st Century*, London: Bloomsbury, 1990, pp. 96–7.

11 Jack Mendelsohn, 'Not in our interest . . . : the ramifications of current US security policy', report of the conference 'Does the Rule of Law Matter?', organized by Just Defence and the Institute for Law and Peace, November 2004, pp. 12–13.

12 Mendelshohn, 'Not in our interest'.

13 Ken Booth, 'Britain's nuclear policy', report of the conference 'Does the rule of law matter?', p. 18, organized by Just Defence and the Institute for Law and Peace, November 2004.

14 Schell, *The Gift of Time*, p. xii.

15 Anthony Kempster, 'Just war or no war?: a view of the transatlantic dialogue', *The Price of Peace. The Anglican Peacemaker 5,*

Milton Keynes: Anglican Pacifist Fellowship, 2005, pp. 2–11.

16 *The Church and the Bomb*, p. 163.

17 *The Church and the Bomb*, p. 147.

18 Martin Luther King, *The Autobiography of Martin Luther King, Jr.*, ed. Clayborne Carson, London: Little, Brown and Co, 1999, p. 27.

19 Yogesh Chadna, *Rediscovering Gandhi*, London: Century, 1997, pp. 366–7.

20 James Howard Kunstler, *The Long Emergency: Surviving the Converging Catastrophes of the Twenty-first Century*, London: Atlantic Books, 2005.

21 Joseph Rotblat, Jack Steinberger and Bhalchandra Udgaonkar (eds), *A Nuclear-weapon-free World: Desirable? Feasible?* Oxford: Westview Press, 1993.

22 Timothy Ferris, 'Keep up the search', *New Scientist*, 22 October 2005.

23 Joe Roeber, 'Parallel markets: corruption in the international arms trade', Campaign Against Arms Trade annual lecture, CAAT: London, 2005.

24 Oliver O'Donovan, *The Just War Revisited*, Cambridge: Cambridge University Press, 2003, pp. ix, 2.

25 Ched Myers, 'Gospel discernment in the apocalypse of war: resisting the propaganda of empire then and now', talk at the 2004 Greenbelt meeting 'Freedom bound', *The Anglican Peacemaker* 4:4, Milton Keynes: Anglican Pacifist Fellowship, 2004, pp. 1–8.

26 Richard Friedman, *The Disappearance of God: A Divine Mystery*, London: The Softback Preview, 1997.

27 Karen Armstrong, *A Short History of Myth*, Edinburgh: Canongate, 2005, pp. 111–13.

## *Chapter 12*

1 Tim Hare, 'What Next for Trident?', *RUSI Journal*, April 2005, p. 30.

2 Max Hastings, 'New weapons, old wars', *The Sunday Telegraph*, 31 July 2005.

3 Hugh Beach and Nadine Gurr, *Flattering the passions: or, the bomb and Britain's bid for a world role*, London: I. B. Tauris, 1999, p. 78.

4 Fred Mulley, 'The politics of Western defence', London: Thames and Hudson, 1962, pp. 45 and 123.

5 Hansard, Column 1133W.

# Notes

6 Otfried Nassauer, 'NATO's nuclear posture review: should Europe end nuclear sharing', BITS Policy Note 02.1, Berlin Information Centre for Transnational Security, April 2002. The costs of the weapons, aircraft and bunkers are, of course, 'sunk'. Costs of training and custody are recurrent.

7 Hansard, Column 602W.

8 'Nuclear Posture Review', see www.globalsecurity.org/wmd/library/policy/dod/npr.htm

9 See www.globalsecurity.org/wmd/library/policy/dod/jp3_12fc2.pdf

10 *The Nuclear Information Project,* nuclear brief, 2 February 2006. See http://www.nukestrat.com/us/jcs/canceled.htm

11 'Nuclear posture review', p. 46.

12 Mark Bromley, David Grahame and Christine Kucia, 'Bunker busters: Washington's drive for new nuclear weapons', BASIC Research Report 2002.2, July 2002, p. 43, http://www.basicint.org/pubs/Research/2002BB.pdf

13 Steven Weinberg, 'The growing nuclear danger', *The New York Review of Books,* 18 July 2002, www.nybooks.com/articles/15604

14 'Nuclear Posture Review', p. 47.

15 Senator Pete Domenici, chair of the subcommittee that oversees the Energy Department's budget, quoted by *CNN* on 25 October 2005.

16 'Nuclear Posture Review', pp. 47–48.

17 Steven Weinberg, 'The growing nuclear danger', *The New York Review of Books,* 18 July 2002, p. 38, www.nybooks.com/articles/15604

18 'Rethinking the unthinkable', *The Economist,* 28 January 2006, pp. 51, 52.

19 Beach and Gurr, *Flattering the passions,* chapter 2.

20 Frank N. von Hippel, 'Does the US need new nuclear weapons', *Physics and Society,* Vol. 31, No. 3, July 2002, p. 4.

21 Nicholas D. Kristof, 'Flirting with disaster: nuclear talk harms the US', *International Herald Tribune,* 15–16 February 2003.

22 MOD Report and Accounts 2004–5, October 2005, para. 75, see http://www.mod.uk/publications/modara04-05/index.html

23 Statement on the Defence Estimates 1994.

24 Malcolm Rifkind, 'UK defence strategy: a continuing role for nuclear weapons', speech to the Centre for Defence Studies, London on 16 November 1993. See *Brassey's Defence Yearbook 1994,* Brasseys, 1994, chapter 1.

25 'Minutes of evidence taken before the Defence Committee', HC 138-II, of session 1998–99, p. 16, para. 180.

26 Michael Quinlan, 'Nuclear weapons and the abolition of war',

address given to the Soviet General Staff in Moscow in November 1990. *International Affairs*, Vol. 2, No. 67, 1991, pp. 293–301. Compare the French notion of 'non-use' (*non-emploi*), as explained by David Fisher in his chapter in this book.

27  Speech at Brest on 19 January 2006. See Ariane Bernard, 'Chirac threatens atom arms on terror', *International Herald Tribune,* 20 January 2006; *The Week*, 28 January 2006, p. 7.

28  *Jonathan Dimbleby Programme*, London Weekend Television, 24 March 2002.

29  Written answer, 17 November 2003. See also Roland Smith's chapter in this book.

30  The assurance reads as follows: 'The United Kingdom will not use nuclear weapons against non-nuclear weapon states party to the Treaty on the Non-Proliferation of Nuclear Weapons except in the case of an invasion or any other attack on the United Kingdom, its dependent territories, its armed forces or other troops, its allies or on a State towards which it has a security commitment, carried out or sustained by such a non-nuclear weapon state in association or alliance with a nuclear-weapon state.' See UN Security Council resolution 984, 11 April 1995.

31  Written questions, 20 June 2005, Column 666W. For a fuller account of the government's present intentions see House of Commons Hansard Debates, oral questions, 23 January 2006, Columns 1151–4.

32  Or buying new ones.

33  Colin Brown, Deputy Political Editor, *The Independent*, 1 November 2005.

34  Andrew Gilligan, *The Spectator*, 29 October 2005.

## Chapter 13

1  The CD (Conference on Disarmament), established in 1979 as the single multilateral disarmament negotiating forum of the international community, was a result of the first Special Session on Disarmament of the UN General Assembly, held in 1978. It succeeded earlier Geneva-based fora.

## Technical Annex

1  See http://www.devonport.co.uk/about-toplevel.htm. HMS *Vanguard* was refitted between February 2002 and January 2005. HMS *Victorious* then began refit.

2  Spearfish is a wire guided torpedo with both active and passive homing and a range of 65 km.

3 The latest development of PWR would allow submarines to circumnavigate the earth 40 times without re-fuelling.

4 This presumably means that no targets have been pre-loaded onto the missiles. The Defence Secretary is on record that 'missiles can be targeted in sufficient time to meet any foreseeable requirement' (House of Commons Hansard written answers, 27 October 2005, No. 21903).

5 A telescoping outward extension that halves frontal drag.

6 Say, ten times faster than *Concord*.

7 For the US, the START I treaty limits this to eight.

8 All the aim-points, however, must lie within an ellipse called a 'footprint'. Its size depends on the range and loft of the missiles' trajectory and is measured in hundreds of nautical miles.

9 These consist of dummy RVs designed to give the same radar signature (size and speed) as real ones, and chaff to blanket radar transmissions.

10 It can be checked by GPS, but this requires an aerial to be raised above water which could compromise the submarine's position, and in war the satellites might already have been knocked out. If operating in a pre-surveyed area, bathymetric data can provide an additional fix.

11 This allows both for the variations in the earth's gravity due to its not being a perfect sphere and for the gravitational effects of the moon.

12 Also confusingly known as the UK Trident Re-entry Body (RB). Its alphanumeric code name has not been released.

13 This figure has never been officially confirmed for British Trident, but appears to be generally accepted as accurate.

14 Public Records Office, Operational Selection Policy, OSP 11, Nuclear Weapons Policy 1967–1998.

15 A reasonable guess would make it 6 feet long with a base diameter of about 2 feet.

16 In American English the word 'pit' means the stone of a fruit.

17 This shell, which can also consist of uranium or tungsten, is usually known as the 'tamper'.

18 One nano-second equals one billionth of a second.

19 The nucleus of an atom of hydrogen contains one proton: the nucleus of deuterium contains a proton and one neutron: tritium has a proton and two neutrons.

20 Also known as a 'tamper'.

21 Rather misleadingly this is normally known as the 'Spark Plug'.

22 The largest thermonuclear explosion ever created by man was the Tsar-Bomba detonated by the Soviet Union in October 1961. This had an explosive yield of 50 megatons and the entire fission–fusion process lasted only 39 nanoseconds.

23 Confirmed most recently by Defence Secretary John Reid in

October 2005, House of Commons Hansard written answers, 27 October 2005, No. 21903.

24 Given that the US is required by the START I Treaty to put no more than eight warheads on each missile, the latter loading (4 x 12) is ruled out for American Trident and is therefore most unlikely to have been adopted by the British.

25 'UK Defence Strategy: a continuing role for nuclear weapons?' Speech to the Centre for Defence Studies, London, 16 November 1993. *Brassey's Defence Yearbook 1994*, Brassey's, 1994, pp. 21–35.

26 Rear Admiral Irwin, MoD Chief Executive, Strategic Systems, in remarks made to the Defence Committee, said that a missile with a single warhead could be used in either a sub-strategic or strategic role. 'Progress of the Trident Programme', 2nd Report of the Defence Committee 1993–4, 4 May 1994, HC 297, p. 26.

27 Commander Tom Herman, 1 Submarine Squadron, Navy News Clyde Supplement, May 1996.

28 'The UK has some flexibility in the choice of yield for the warheads on its Trident missiles', Defence Secretary George Robertson in the House of Commons, *Hansard*, 19 March 1998, column 724.

29 See note 26.

30 *Ibid.*

31 One speculation, by the Bulletin of Atomic Scientists, runs as follows: 'Some Trident II SLBMs have a single warhead and are assigned targets once covered by WE177 gravity bombs. For example, when the *Vigilant* is on patrol, 10, 12, or 14 of its SLBMs may carry up to three warheads per missile, but the other two, four, or six missiles may be armed with just one warhead'. See http://www.thebulletin.org/article_nn.php?art_ofn=ja99norris

32 Polaris missiles in the first instance. These were replaced by Trident missiles in the 1990s as explained above.

33 The text of the Nassau agreement was given in the White Paper Cmnd 1915 and published in *The Times*, 22 December 1962.

34 Ministry of Defence, *Strategic Defence Review*, July 1998, para. 55.

35 The exact wording is 'source, by-product and special nuclear material, and other material for research on, development of or use in atomic weapons, when the Government of the United States . . . determines that the transfer of such material is necessary to improve the United Kingdom's atomic weapon design, development or fabrication capability'.

36 1958 Atomic Energy Agreement, *UN Treaty Series*, No. 4707, Vol. 326, 1959, pp. 4–20, amendment. *UN Treaty Series*, No. 4707, Vol. 351, 1960, pp. 458–64.

37 Message to Congress from President Bush, 14 June 2004. See http://www.whitehouse.gov

38 The main difference is the Trident submarines have 16 missile tubes while the Ohio Class has 24.

39 The barter also included the transfer of some 6.7 kilogrammes of tritium from the US to the UK. Information release by the US Department of Energy, 22 December 1997.

40 See http://tx.mb21.co.uk/features/skelton/index.asp

41 This would not, of course, apply to Trident used in a sub-strategic role.

42 Satellite Communications Acquisition IPT. IPT 133. www.mod.uk/linked_files/dpa/satsynop2.pdf. It is known that this system is being acquired for British Astute Class submarines, but the MoD has said that there is no current requirement for terminals to be fitted to Trident Boats. Letter from head of DCSA Secretariat, 1 February 2006.

43 This will be fully compatible with GPS, and will provide world-wide cover, giving accuracy within one metre, readable by a small cheap individual receiver.

44 With current ship-based methods it would apparently take 200 years to survey the bed of all the oceans in the world.

45 Defence Secretary John Reid, House of Commons Hansard written answers for 27 October 2005.

46 www.subasekb.navy.mil/TRIDENT%20REFIT%20FACILITY/MISSION.htm. This website claims that the Trident Refit Facility provides 'total integrated logistical supply support to attack and UK submarines' including degaussing services.

47 See http://www.lockheedmartin.com/wms/findPage.do?dsp=fec&ci==12336&rsbci=0&fti=0&ti=0&sc=400=fec&ci&prfr=true

48 See http://www.jhuapl.edu/newscenter/aplupdate/pdf/upo01017.pdf

49 At a cost of some $47 million. Adam Ingram, Armed Forces Minister, in House of Commons *Hansard*, written answer, 18 June 2004.

50 Originally California Analysis Centre Inc.

51 CACI News Release, 10 May 2002.

52 For 'Insert Word' message see under 'Target Planning and Fire Control' above. The contract reference is 'FY05 Mod5 UK Intent Word Displays, Award N0030002G0054NJ72'.

53 http://www.awe.co.uk/main_site/about_awe/ click on logo for AWE's Annual Report 2004, pp. 4–5.

54 http://www.sandia.gov/LabNews/LN03-07-03/LA2003/la03/nuclear_story.htm

55 The British explosive, known as EDC37, has the same base explo-

sive but in finer particles and a softer binder. This means that the way the primary operates will not be identical and separate safety assessments are needed of responses to shock and heat.

56 For 30 years between 1962 and 1991 British scientists conducted 24 nuclear tests with their US colleagues at the Nevada Test Site. The last live test of a British warhead took place on 26 November 1991, www.thebulletin.org/article_nn.php?art_ofn=ndo5norris

57 'We have declared the strategic system to NATO and we plan and de-conflict our NATO plans with the targeting centre in Omaha'. Admiral Irwin, 'Progress of Trident', 6th Report, Defence Select Committee 1993, HC549, minutes of meeting 10 March 1993, para. 1573.

58 Lord Henley, House of Lords, 11 January 1995.

59 c.f. Defence Secretary Robert McNamara in 1962 who declared such systems to be dangerous.

60 House of Commons *Hansard*, 6 June 2005, [1925], col. 987.

61 Tim Hare, 'What next for Trident?', *RUSI Journal*, April 2005, pp. 30–3.

62 The Royal Navy claims that a British submarine on deterrent patrol has never been detected.

63 http://www.fas.org/nuke/guide/usa/slbm/ssbn-726.htm

64 Defence Secretary Geoff Hoon, House of Commons *Hansard*, written answer, 30 June 2004.

65 Facilities at Aldermaston and Burghfield are being upgraded at a cost of £350 million for each of the next three years. Ostensibly this is to provide assurance of continued reliability and safety for the existing warhead stock, since live nuclear testing is no longer allowed under the Comprehensive Test Ban Treaty, of which the UK is a party. But it also helps to keep the British up to speed *vis-à-vis* the Americans in the art of new warhead design. MoD Press Release, 146/2005, 19 July 2005.

66 It is generally accepted that during the Cold War the British Strategic Nuclear Missile Force was sized so as to pose an effective threat to Moscow, as protected by Anti-Ballistic Missile defences. This no doubt applied to the decision to acquire the Trident D5 missile, taken in 1981. The reduced numbers described in this Annex derived from the *Strategic Defence Review 1998*, chapter 4, pp. 17, 18.

67 This could go as low as one missile carrying one warhead, by way of *reductio ad absurdum*!

68 Some 367 missiles in all.

69 Tim Hare, as in footnote 61 above.

70 There is evidence that the last three live nuclear tests of British warheads were for this project, not Trident.

71 According to John Ainslie, a complete rebuild of a Trident-like

system would cost over £15 billion at present prices. This sounds on the cheap side. Each individual submarine would cost more than £1 billion. 'The future of the British Bomb', WMD Awareness Programme, October 2005, p. 26.

72 Richard Scott, 'Interview with Admiral Sir Alan West', *Jane's Defence Weekly*, 8 February 2006.